salads

salads
appetizers, entrées, and sides

Elsa Petersen-Schepelern

photography by Peter Cassidy

RYLAND
PETERS
& SMALL
LONDON NEW YORK

Dedicated to Ron and Kirsten Bray

Senior Designer Susan Downing

Editors Katherine Steer, Susan Stuck

Production Patricia Harrington

Art Director Gabriella Le Grazie

Publishing Director Alison Starling

Food Stylist Linda Tubby

Prop Stylist Róisín Nield

Indexer Hilary Bird

Published in the United States in 2003
by Ryland Peters & Small, Inc.
519 Broadway, 5th Floor, New York, NY 1001
www.rylandpeters.com

10 9 8 7 6 5 4 3 2 1

Library of Congress Cataloging-in-Publication Data
Petersen-Schepelern, Elsa.
  Salads : appetizers, entrées, and sides / Elsa Petersen-Schepelern ;
photography by Peter Cassidy.
    p. cm.
Includes bibliographical references and index.
  ISBN 1-84172-424-6
  1. Salads. I. Title.
  TX740 . P467 2003
  641.8'3--dc21
                                        2002152845

Printed and bound in China.

Notes All spoon measurements are level.

All eggs are large, unless otherwise specified. Uncooked or partially cooked eggs
should not be served to the very young, the very old, those with compromised
immune systems, or to pregnant women.

Author's Acknowledgments As usual, I would like to thank Pete Cassidy, Linda
Tubby, and Róisín Nield for their beautiful work. Thanks also to nephews Peter Bray
and Luc Votan, and to Susan, Martin, Tessa, Karen, and Mike, who have tasted
their way through the testing. Friends and fellow food writers have also been
generous with their time and advice—Clare Ferguson, Sonia Stevenson, Alastair
Hendy, Louise Pickford, Kimiko Barber, and Linda Tubby among others. As usual,
many thanks. My grateful thanks also to my editors, Kathy Steer, Susan Stuck, and
Roy Butcher—plus designer Susan Downing, who is terrific fun as well.

contents

not just greens ...

Everyone loves a salad. It's one of the world's most versatile dishes. You can serve something small, light, and elegant as an appetizer, something substantial and satisfying as an entrée, or something contrasting and crunchy as a side dish.

For elegant dinner parties, the salad often followed the entrée in order to clear the palate, vying for position with the cheese, which the French serve after the entrée to accompany any remaining red wine. The English serve it after as well, because if it's a green salad, some people like to mix the dressing with the meat juices. The rest of us please ourselves, and our meals are surely the more delicious because of it.

It's odd to think that the word is derived from the Latin *sal* (salt). The Romans ate vegetables and leaves with a simple dressing of salt, oil, or vinegar—similar to the way they do today, in dishes like *pinzimonio* (crudités with vinaigrette). That may be why we identify dishes dressed with these three items as "salads" when they appear in other cuisines. The Japanese serve *aemono* and *sunomono*, or "little vinegared things," in tiny, elegant bowls. The Vietnamese have a passion for huge plates of herbs, "table salads," which are added to many dishes. A true Vietnamese salad—or one from other countries in the region—is often dressed with fish sauce (the salt element), and lime juice (the vinegar element). Often the oil element is missing, so we can congratulate ourselves on a healthy, low-fat salad whenever we serve one of these salads.

In this book, I've tried to give you a taste of salads from around the world, as well as information on preparing them that I must admit is hugely opinionated, but I hope useful to you, since it is certainly based on lots of eating experience.

the basics

greens

choosing

Once, lettuces came in one variety—iceberg. Now, there are dozens of different greens. Choose the one best suited to the other ingredients in the salad, or in the rest of the meal, or to your own inclinations and those of your family and friends. There are four general categories of greens; sweet and soft, crisp and crunchy, bitter, or spicy.

• Sweet and soft leaves include Bibb and Boston lettuce, lamb's lettuce (mâche or corn salad), oakleaf, and mignonettes (cut-and-come-again lettuces).

• Crisp, crunchy leaves include iceberg and romaine.

• The bitter category includes greens such as frisée, baby spinach, radicchio, escarole, and endive.

• Hot, spicy notes are provided by watercress, arugula, and nasturtium leaves and flowers, for instance.

preparation

I think one of the world's great inventions has been the salad spinner. Before I was given one, I used to wash greens in a bowl, drain them in a colander, then wrap them in a dish towel, go outside, and sling my arm in circles as if I were making billy tea, a famous and undrinkable Australian beverage.

Now, I put them in the spinner, put the cage in the sink, wash them thoroughly, give them a few twirls, and they're perfect. That is unless they have very tender leaves, when gentler treatment is needed.

I was delighted when supermarkets introduced bags of ready-washed mixed greens, often labeled "mesclun." The only problem is I suddenly thought "What have they been washed in, and exactly what sort of air is in the bag with them if they don't wilt like normal lettuce leaves."

So, I wash them anyway, like a racoon, but I do it at the very last minute and let them drain on paper towels.

Jennifer Patterson, she of the Two Fat Ladies, kept her bowl of salad leaves out on the fire escape until she was ready to serve. That's fine if you live in a cold climate, and your fire escape has signed up to the Clean Air Act. However, Jennifer was absolutely right—a bit of chill will certainly perk them up.

windowboxes and flowerpots

Food writers and celebrity chefs often surprise us with unusual and hard-to-buy greens, herbs, and vegetables. These are the people responsible for introducing us to interesting and delicious ingredients—ingredients that, inevitably, become accepted day-to-day foods. In some places, even olive oil wasn't widely available until about 20 years ago, and there was a time when arugula wasn't found even in speciality greengrocers, let alone a regular supermarket.

For today's home cooks, at least in the salad and herb department, it is possible to grow your own. You don't need a huge garden to do it, either. A couple of flowerpots or windowboxes are perfectly adequate for most of our needs—and the quality of freshly picked produce is a revelation.

A windowbox with herbs like thyme, oregano, parsley, chives, and rosemary will be very useful. Most of them, thankfully,

rather like dry, sunny conditions. You can also sow arugula seeds in a flowerpot, for an ongoing supply of baby leaves. In addition, interesting Japanese herbs and leaves are now sold by speciality seed suppliers. Seed and plant suppliers are now readily accessible online and via mail order. See page 126 for contact details.

salad safety

What? Salads a safety hazard? Who would ever have believed it? However, salad ingredients are just as prone to mishaps as any other food, especially because some of them are cooked, then cooled, and this can be a trap.

Lettuces and other vegetables grow in or near the ground. And soil, let's face it, is dirt. You don't know where it's been. So just wash it off thoroughly, then rinse and dry before using. That looks after dirt. What about pesticides and other baddies

inflicted on the vegetable world by humans? My solution is to go for organically grown and pesticide-free produce. I prefer to buy eggs, meat, and poultry that has been raised kindly and free range.

There are some foods especially prone to spoiling after cooking. Chicken, for instance, should be cooked thoroughly and, in my view, served in a salad as soon as it's cool enough to handle. Even meats that can be served rare, like beef and

duck, are better warm or just cool (page 17). Interestingly, smoked items, which were originally smoked to preserve them, don't last as long because the producers know they'll be kept in the refrigerator.

The surprise culprit, however, is rice. Many of us would never think of rice as dangerous, but cooked rice spoils very quickly. However, one of the best tricks I know is to stir sushi vinegar dressing through it—this will keep it fresh for up to a day (page 125).

oils, vinegars, and juices

about oils

I can be infinitely pedantic about oils—you have been warned.

- Oils are better for you if they are extracted without the use of heat.

- Oils are fats—and some fats are better for you than others. Cold-pressed olive, avocado, sunflower, safflower, and peanut oils are good, but corn oil and vegetable oil less so. I use butter or ghee, but never margarine.

- Fats are not necessarily bad for you—they are necessary for hormones of all kinds, for brain function, and for the proper development of babies.

- When heated, fats change to become more dangerous—all except butter. So—amazing though it may seem, butter is actually an excellent cooking medium. And it tastes wonderful.

salad oils

- For regular salads, cold-pressed extra virgin olive oil is the best. But it has an assertive flavor. That flavor is an advantage for most foods—but for a less pronounced taste, choose a blander oil, such as peanut, sunflower, or safflower. Cold pressed of course.

- For Asian salads, you will find that oil is very often omitted in favor of other flavors, such as citrus juices, rice vinegars, wines and spirits, salt and its derivatives, such as soy sauce or fish sauce, or other fruit juices, such as tamarind or plum.

- Sesame oil, toasted or not, should be used as a seasoning note—not as a major ingredient. Use just a few drops with other oils. I think it goes well with watercress.

- My other favorite seed oil is pumpkin seed, but it becomes rancid very quickly. The bottles I buy are quite large, so I decant them into smaller bottles, cork firmly, and keep in a cool dark place. I am currently trying the refrigerator.

nut oils

- My favorites are walnut oil, hazelnut oil, and macadamia oil, but used in a ratio of about 3 parts olive oil to 1 part nut oil, otherwise they're too assertive.

- Nut oils, like seed oils, turn rancid hugely quickly. I always buy in tiny bottles, preferably for a particular recipe which includes the nut in question.

about vinegars

Vinegar forms a counterpoint to the smoothness of oils—and is sometimes used by itself.

- Wine vinegar—red and white—goes with most European dressings, especially those from wine-producing areas such as those bordering the Mediterranean.

- I prefer white wine vinegar. Red wine vinegar is stronger and discolors food. It may depend on your own taste.

- Champagne is just a more delicate form of white wine vinegar, and its appeal may have more to do with the romance of its name than its inherent properties.

- Sherry vinegar, on the other hand, is a much more complex and interesting flavor. One of my favorites.

- Cider vinegar is made from cider apples, and has a sweet and attractive flavor.

- Rice vinegars are very useful in salads—mild and often complex. Dark vinegars are not entirely suitable for salads, since they often have caramel added.

- Balsamic vinegar is, very often, a fraud. True balsamic is aged for years, and is very expensive. Inexpensive balsamic has, almost certainly, been made of regular vinegar with caramel added. To improve its flavor, Sydney food writer Louise Pickford reduces it by boiling it down by about two-thirds (see recipe page 21).

- I have never been a fan of fruit vinegars, such as raspberry, or herb vinegars, such as tarragon, believing that the fresh herb added will have more interest than an acidified old leaf. But if you like them, do use them.

about juices

- Lemon and lime juice can take the place of vinegars in salad dressings, and are widely used in Southeast Asia with salt, sugar, and spicy ingredients.

- Orange juice will perform the same function as wine vinegar, and is often used in Moroccan salads.

- Japanese umeboshi plum vinegar is divine in salads. Sweet but sharp, it has an elusive flavor that is suitable for salads other than Japanese (see page 56).

preparing protein

How many times have you been presented with the salad version of the rubber chicken? One of the reasons it's like that is that it has been refrigerated and not brought back to room temperature before serving. That's understandable, perhaps, in a large catering establishment, but when you cook at home you can prepare these ingredients in the most delicious way.

chicken

Roast, poach, or steam the chicken in the usual way, let cool a little, then pull the flesh off the bones, in big pieces. Chicken will taste better, with better texture, if pulled, not cut, into smaller pieces. It will taste better if you don't refrigerate it, so if you can make the salad as soon as it's cool enough to handle, or at room temperature, the flavor and texture will always be better. However, if you're keeping it for any length of time, health concerns dictate that it must be refrigerated. Return it to room temperature before serving.

duck

I pan-grill the breasts, skin side down, at low-medium heat until the fat has almost completely rendered out, about 20 minutes. Pour off the fat from time to time. Season the flesh side, then turn and cook the flesh side just until browned. The skin should be crisp, the fat mostly rendered and the flesh pinkly rare. I like the legs to be roasted until the skin is crispy, then pull the skin and flesh into shreds. This treatment is especially good for Asian salads.

beef

Beef for salads is best cooked rare, then carved into thick slices and served warm or cool. Again, refrigerators solidify the fat in meat or poultry and make it less palatable.

chickpeas, and dried peas, beans, and lentils

These ingredients are just made for the salad treatment. I defy anyone not to have opened a convenient can, then rinsed, drained, and dressed the contents. However, the canned versions often contain both sugar and salt, and are also more expensive than the dried versions. It would be great to be able to give a schedule for how long each kind should be soaked, then how long they should be boiled, but it really depends how old they were to start with, and how long they'd been kept. Keeping a long time doesn't mean they're not as good—it just takes longer to cook them. There are several golden rules:

• Don't presoak lentils. No need—they cook in a very short time anyway.

• To soak peas and beans, put them in a bowl, cover with cold water, and soak for 8 hours or overnight. To save time, cover with boiling water and let soak for about 2 hours before cooking.

• Never add salt until the end of cooking, or about 5 minutes from the end. If you do, they'll take forever to cook: in fact, you can throw away the beans and eat the pan.

• Always preboil red beans for 10 minutes or so before you start to cook them. Throw away the water and start again. This is true particularly for red kidney beans, but I apply it to any red bean.

preparing dressings

Although this book isn't a compendium of every salad and every dressing ever known, there are a few hobby-horses I would like to put over the jumps.

• Why on earth does anyone ever make a dressing in a bottle—or keep it for later? The simplest way to make a vinaigrette is to put the ingredients in the salad bowl and beat them with a fork. Put the leaves on top, toss them with your hands (clean I would assume), or, if you're very dainty, a couple of spoons. Hands are kinder, and you can make sure every leaf is lightly covered with oil. It takes absolutely no time, and you don't have unpleasant bottles of dregs lurking about in the refrigerator.

• Some salads with very tender leaves, like mesclun or baby arugula, you might like to dress them at the last minute, perhaps even having your guests add their own. My solution is to mix it and put it in a small pitcher so you can pour it properly.

• So you won't need any screw-top bottles—except for a picnic, when you can take the dressing separately in a screw-top bottle and dress just before serving.

• Italy provides the best idea of all. Like sensible people they have the oil, vinegar, salt, and pepper on the table for people to dress the salad themselves. For an Italian salad, it always seems to work best like this anyway. The order is salt, then vinegar, then oil, tossing between each addition. Then pepper, but if you're in a restaurant, they may not trust you with the pepper grinder—you obviously have to be a sturdy Italian waiter with strong biceps and much charm in order to wield that pepper cudgel.

garlic in dressings

When garlic first dawned on the palates of non-Mediterranean people, we were advised to rub the (wooden) salad bowl with it, so our tastebuds wouldn't get too much of a fright and our breath wouldn't offend. Presumably, the salad bowl soon started to smell of stale garlic.

However, I do think you can overdo garlic in salad dressings, especially at the end of the season, when garlic is very strong and peppery. So that's my rule: late in the season, I use about 1 garlic clove in a salad for 4 people, crushed to a paste with a pinch of salt, before stirring in the other dressing ingredients. In spring, when it's mild and sweet, I use as many as I like.

In fact, spring garlic sliced into a bowl of oil makes a great dip. Cut it across the top into thin slices to produce a beautiful mosaic pattern. Put in a small bowl, cover with oil, sprinkle a few drops of balsamic vinegar on top, followed by sea salt flakes and cracked black pepper. Let infuse for 30 minutes or so before using it as a dip for vegetables—a sort of *pinzimonio balsamico*.

the vinaigrette family

Vinaigrette can be a simple thing—just oil, vinegar, or other acidulator such as citrus juice, plus salt and freshly ground black pepper. You can add lots of other things to ring the changes, but in my opinion, this simple mixture can't be beaten. I think the oil should be as good as you can find, and the vinegar as little as possible. The secret is in the ratio of oil to vinegar. I like the ratio of 6 parts oil to 1 part vinegar, but this can be a matter of taste. I find you can use more if the vinegar is replaced by lemon juice. Remember, if you have to add sugar, you've probably used too much vinegar.

vinaigrette

6 tablespoons extra virgin olive oil
1 tablespoon white wine vinegar
sea salt and freshly ground black pepper

makes about ½ cup

Put the oil, vinegar, salt, and pepper in a salad bowl and beat with a fork or small whisk.

variations

• Add 1 teaspoon Dijon mustard and beat well. The mustard helps form an emulsion.

• Use harissa paste instead of mustard.

• Crush the garlic with a pinch of salt to form a paste.

• I like to use Japanese rice vinegar, which gives a mild, smooth taste. You can also substitute red wine vinegar, sherry vinegar, cider vinegar, or others.

• Use freshly squeezed lime or lemon juice instead of the vinegar.

• Instead of extra virgin, use 2 tablespoons mild virgin olive oil and 3 tablespoons nut oil such as walnut, macadamia, or hazelnut (page 14). Nut oils turn rancid very quickly, so buy small quantities, keep in the refrigerator and use quickly (keep nuts there too).

• Heat the vinaigrette in a small saucepan over gently heat until just warm, then pour over the salad.

• One of the nicest dressings of all is just a sprinkle of the very best quality extra virgin olive oil.

• Amazingly, a simple sprinkling of lemon juice or a mild vinegar is a great dressing for some salads such as tomatoes.

blue cheese dressing

8 oz. Gorgonzola dolcellate, or other blue cheese, crumbled
6 tablespoons extra virgin olive oil
2 tablespoons white wine vinegar
sea salt and freshly ground black pepper

makes about ½ cup

To make the dressing, put the crumbled cheese in a bowl and crush with a fork. Add 2 tablespoons of the olive oil and mash until creamy, adding the remaining olive oil and the vinegar as you go. If the end result is too thick, beat in a little hot water until the mixture is loose and creamy. Add salt and pepper to taste—take care with the salt, because blue cheese is already quite salty.

The dressing will thicken on standing, so you may have beat it again before serving (or you can add a little water to thin it down).

italian dressing

In many Italian restaurants, especially in Italy, you will see a "cruet" of oil and vinegar (below) or just bottles of vinegar and oil, usually from the local area. You dress your salad to taste. First the salt, then vinegar, then the oil.

reduced balsamic vinegar

Sydney food writer Louise Pickford reduces cheap balsamic vinegar to produce a thick dressing, used in drops.

1½ cups balsamic vinegar

makes ½ cup

Put the vinegar in a small saucepan and boil gently until it is reduced by two-thirds and is the consistency of thick syrup. Let cool, then store in a clean bottle. The result can be used in drops as a seasoning.

the mayonnaise family

The key to making mayonnaise is to have all the ingredients at room temperature, and to add the oil a few drops at a time at first, then more quickly, but not in a continuous stream as many books advise. The emulsion needs time to absorb the oil, so don't overtax it. Don't use all olive oil (unless you're making aïoli)—the flavor is too strong. Use a light oil, such as safflower, but good quality: don't use those labeled just "vegetable oil," because they have usually been heat-extracted. I prefer a food processor to make mayonnaise but, if you're a purist, by all means make it by hand.

classic mayonnaise

2 egg yolks, at room temperature

1 whole egg (if making in a food processor)

2 teaspoons Dijon mustard

a large pinch of salt

2 teaspoons freshly squeezed lemon juice or white wine vinegar

1 cup good-quality sunflower, safflower, or peanut oil (not corn oil)

½ cup virgin olive oil

makes about 2 cups

If making in a food processor, put the egg yolks, whole egg, mustard, salt and lemon juice in the bowl and blend until pale. If making by hand, omit the whole egg. Gradually add the oil, a few drops at a time at first, then more quickly, but in stages, leaving a few seconds between additions to allow the eggs to "digest" the oil. When all the oil has been added, if the mixture is too thick, add 1 tablespoon warm water. Serve immediately, or press plastic wrap over the surface to prevent

a skin from forming. The mayonnaise may be refrigerated for up to 3 days.

aïoli

An unctuous garlic mayonnaise served with Provençal dishes such as Le Grand Aïoli on page 48. Crush 4 garlic cloves and put in a food processor at the same time as the eggs. Proceed as in the main recipe, using all olive oil. In spring, you can use more garlic than later in the season.

rouille aïoli

Add 1 tablespoon harissa paste at the end of the recipe to make a quick rouille with a North African accent.

potato salad dressing

¾ cup light cream

½ recipe Classic Mayonnaise (left)

1 tablespoon Dijon mustard

makes about 1½ cups

Stir the cream into the mayonnaise to thin it a little, then stir in the mustard. This should only be done with homemade mayonnaise. Alternatively, omit the cream and use a whole recipe of mayonnaise.

thousand island dressing

An American classic, good with cold meats.

¾ cup Classic Mayonnaise (left)

¼ cup low-fat yogurt

3 tablespoons chile sauce

½ green bell pepper, finely chopped

½ red bell pepper, roasted and finely chopped

1 teaspoon finely grated onion

makes about 2 cups

Put the mayonnaise and yogurt into a bowl. Add the chile sauce, peppers, and onion and stir well. Serve immediately or cover and refrigerate for up to 8 hours.

green goddess dressing

Another great American dressing.

2 cups Classic Mayonnaise (left)

8 canned anchovy fillets, drained and mashed with a fork

2 scallions, green and white, chopped

a bunch of chives, snipped

a handful of parsley, chopped

2 tablespoons chopped fresh tarragon

¼ cup tarragon vinegar

makes about 3 cups

Put all the ingredients in a bowl and stir well. Serve immediately or cover and refrigerate for up to 8 hours.

variation

Put 1–2 cups mayonnaise in a food processor. Add 4 anchovies, 2 tablespoons each of tarragon, parsley, and chives, 1 tablespoon lemon juice, and 3 tablespoons vinegar, salt, and pepper. Process until smooth.

the pesto family

Although in Italy pesto is only used with pasta, the rest of us have fallen in love with it. It makes a delicious addition to salad—potato, tomato, chickpeas, and beans—stirred through rice or couscous with extra herbs.

basil pesto

¼ cup pine nuts

4 garlic cloves, crushed

1 teaspoon sea salt

a large double handful of basil leaves

1 oz. freshly grated Parmesan cheese

½ cup extra virgin olive oil, or to taste

makes about 1 cup

Put the pine nuts in a dry skillet and sauté gently and quickly until golden (about 30 seconds). They burn very easily, so don't leave them. Let cool. Transfer to a food processor or blender, add the garlic, salt, and basil, and blend to a paste. Add the Parmesan, blend again, then add the oil and blend again until smooth. Add extra oil if you want a looser texture.

parsley pesto

Make basil in full summer, when the leaves are big and full of their sweet, strong flavor. At other times, make a milder pesto using parsley, preferably the Italian flat-leaf variety.

arugula pesto

Use half parsley and half arugula leaves.

red pesto

Instead of basil, use 8 oz. semi-dried tomatoes (or sun-dried tomatoes bottled in olive oil, but drained). A teaspoon of harissa paste lifts the flavor even further.

cilantro pesto

Use cilantro instead of basil, peanut or safflower oil instead of olive, 1 garlic clove, a squeeze of lemon or lime juice, and (optional) grated fresh ginger.

asian dressings

southeast asian dressings

Although Southeast Asia has created dozens of dressings, those without oil appeal to me most. They include salt, sour, sweet, and hot elements, and cooks add a little more of one or less of another according to their taste, traditions, and the flavor and texture of what they're dressing. In Vietnam especially, salt components don't appear on the table, so it's up to the cook to decide. The one element the diners are trusted to add to taste is chile. That said, in some Thai restaurants, it's common with some dishes (not usually salads) to be given a "cruet" set of grated palm sugar, crushed dried chiles, chiles in vinegar and chiles in fish sauce. Fire!

vietnamese chile-lime dressing

You will notice that there is quite a lot of brown sugar in this one, because of the large quantity of chile and ginger. Before the Portuguese took chiles to Asia, pepper and ginger alone satisfied the appetite for hot, spicy tastes. Now you can't think of Asia without chiles.

6 tablespoons lime juice, 2–3 limes

1 tablespoon fish sauce

2 tablespoons brown sugar

2 chiles, seeded and finely chopped

1 garlic clove, crushed

1 inch fresh ginger, peeled and grated

makes about ¾ cup

Put all the ingredients in a bowl and beat well until the sugar has dissolved.

thai fresh chilli dressing

4 tablespoons lime juice

2 tablespoons fish sauce

2 bird chiles, seeded and chopped

Put the lime juice, fish sauce, and chiles in a bowl and stir.

spicy thai dressing

¼ cup fish sauce

freshly squeezed juice of 1 lemon or 2 limes

2 teaspoons brown sugar

2 tablespoons red Thai curry paste

makes about ½ cup

Put the fish sauce, lime or lemon juice, sugar, and curry paste in a bowl and beat with a fork.

sesame oil dressing

1 inch fresh ginger, peeled and sliced

3 scallions, chopped

1 red chile, seeded and chopped

1 tablespoon peppercorns, preferably Szechuan

¾ cup peanut oil

¼ cup sesame oil

makes about 1½ cups

Put the ginger, scallions, chile, and peppercorns in a small blender and pulse to chop. Put the peanut and sesame oils in a saucepan and heat until hot but not smoking. Remove from the heat, add the flavorings, stir, cover with a lid, let cool, then strain. Serve tossed through blanched vegetables, chicken, or noodle salads.

lime dressing

1 tablespoon fish sauce

freshly squeezed juice of 1 lime

1 teaspoon brown sugar

makes about ¼ cup

Mix in a small bowl and serve as a dipping sauce, or sprinkled over a salad.

peanut sauce

8 oz. shelled raw peanuts (1½ cups)

2 red chiles, seeded and thinly sliced

2 bird chiles, seeded and thinly sliced

1 onion, finely chopped

1 garlic clove, crushed

1 teaspoon sea salt

2 teaspoons brown sugar

¾ cup canned coconut milk

serves 4–8

Toast the peanuts in a dry skillet. Transfer to a clean, dry dish towel, rub off the skins, then put the nuts in a blender. Grind to a coarse meal, then add the chiles, onion, garlic, salt, sugar, and coconut milk. Blend to a purée, then transfer to a saucepan and cook, stirring, until thickened. When ready to serve, thin with water to a pourable consistency.

japanese dressings

Japanese salads usually involve just one or two ingredients, simply dressed, served in small quantities, beautifully arranged in small bowls, heaped in a mountain shape.

sambai-zu

This is a popular everyday Japanese salad dressing, used in many homes. Sweet, salty, and sour.

3 tablespoons rice vinegar

1 teaspoon tamari soy sauce

1 tablespoon white sugar

a pinch of salt

makes about 6 tablespoons

Put all the ingredients in a bowl and beat with a fork. Spoon over the salad.

kimi-zu

A Japanese version of mayonnaise, again salty, sweet, and sour.

2 egg yolks

½ teaspoon salt

1½ tablespoons white sugar

½ teaspoon cornstarch

¼ cup dashi stock*

2 tablespoons rice vinegar

makes about ⅔ cup

Put the egg yolks in a heatproof bowl set over a saucepan of simmering water. Beat with a whisk, then beat in the salt, sugar, and cornstarch. Gradually stir in the dashi and vinegar. Continue simmering, stirring, until thickened. The cornstarch will stop it curdling, but don't let the mixture boil.

nihai-zu

A dressing for shellfish and fish salads, like the Crab and Cucumber Salad on page 75.

3 tablespoons white rice vinegar

2 tablespoons tamari soy sauce

a pinch of salt

makes about 5 tablespoons

Put all the ingredients in a bowl and whisk with a fork. Spoon over the salad.

goma-zu

Sesame seed dressing, good for vegetables.

¼ cup black sesame seeds

1 tablespoon sugar

2 tablespoons tamari soy sauce

1 tablespoon sake

2 tablespoons rice vinegar

makes ¾ cup

Toast the sesame seeds in a dry skillet over low heat until aromatic. Using a mortar and pestle, grind to a powder. Add the sugar and grind again, then stir in the soy sauce, sake, and vinegar. If preferred, add 1 tablespoon water or dashi.

ponzu sauce

This fashionable dressing can be difficult to make because yuzu fruit (a kind of citrus fruit) is rare outside Japan. The juice is sometimes available in speciality stores, or can be ordered.

grated zest and juice of 1 yuzu or small blood orange (or Seville)

tamari soy sauce

Put the zest and juice in a bowl, then stir in an equal quantity of soy sauce.

Most common Asian ingredients are now available in larger supermarkets. Japanese ingredients, such as powdered dashi, can be found near the sushi ingredients. Chinese and other Asian markets also sell it in liquid concentrate form.

things on top

four ways with croutons

The traditional way to prepare croutons is to cut thick slices of bread, remove the crusts, then cut the remainder into cubes (day-old bread is best). Heat butter or butter and oil in a skillet, add the cubes, and sauté until golden on all sides. I find that it's too easy to burn them this way.

Alternatively, you put the cubes into a roasting pan, sprinkle with oil, toss to coat, then cook in a preheated oven at 400°F until golden.

A friend of mine toasts the slices in a toaster until pale gold, then cuts the slices into cubes and sautés them in just a little butter and oil until golden.

I always find that my croutons squash into flat squares, not tidy cubes. So—I prefer them more freeform, rough, and ready. I tear good Italian bread into bits, heat a little olive oil in a skillet and sauté until golden on most sides. A little more rustic, but equally delicious. A garlic clove squashed into the cooking oil makes them even better. However, if you prefer traditional, don't let me lead you astray.

salt, sweet, and sour

bacon or prosciutto

There's nothing more delicious than salty, smoky, hot bacon added to a salad. I like to fry regular thinly sliced bacon and crumble it into bits or cut a thick slab of bacon into little lardons and fry them until they're crisp. Of course, there's pancetta (I love the smoky kind) cut into cubes or thinly sliced, or prosciutto in any guise.

anchovies

Anchovy is my favorite salty flavor, along with fish sauce. I use the dry-salted kind, preferably taken from a big can, packed as a wheel, noses in the middle, from an old-fashioned Greek or Italian deli. You have to wash, skin, and bone them yourself. Since such stores are a dying breed, I am usually forced to use the regular canned or bottled fillets. Use them whole, or mash them into the dressing (and don't use any more salt in the salad until you've tasted it).

Anchovies act in much the same way as soy sauce or fish sauce do in Asian cooking—as a salt flavor, but a more interesting, smoky kind of salt.

sugar

In Southeast Asian salads, palm sugar is used to balance the fire of chiles. If you can't find it, use brown instead—I think if you're going to use sugar, it should have more oomph than ordinary white sugar. I don't think you should have to use it in vinaigrettes at all—if you do, you've used too much vinegar.

lemon zest and lime zest

Citrus zest makes and unbeatable addition to all sorts of foods. Think of lime added to tropical flavors and lemon to more temperature ones. Remove the zest in shreds or grate it finely. Whatever you use, invest in a good zester, one that doesn't include the bitter white pith. Even more important is to choose unwaxed fruit, or to wash off the wax with warm water. Be careful—if it's too hot, it will release the essential oils and you'll lose some of the citrus flavor.

One of my favorite versions is the rind of preserved lemons, one of the glories of Moroccan cooking (see recipe on page 80). They are preserved in brine—you discard the flesh and use only the salty skin. Buy them in French or North African gourmet stores.

capers and caperberries

Capers (the buds) and their cousins caperberries (the berries) are one of those love-them-or-hate-them flavors—a mixture of salt and vinegar that appeals to a grownup palate, just like olives, which you hate when you're a child, but learn to love later.

I prefer capers that have been packed in sea salt, rather than those in brine. They are slightly more expensive. You have to rinse off the salt, but you can then make them less salty than regular capers.

olives

Black or green, pitted or not, dry-cured, with flavorings such as herbs, garlic, chiles, or pepper, or stuffed (please not!) with pimentos. I always prefer them with the pits in—in the belief that they taste so much better. If the recipe needs pitted ones, pit them yourself. I like best-quality Kalamata from Greece, Niçoise from the south of France, and anything Italian.

toasted nuts and seeds, and nut or seed oils

Toasted nuts or seeds are a wonderful addition to a salad. But almost any nut or seed will be improved by being lightly toasted in a dry skillet before use. Think of pine nuts, and how amazingly good they taste after this treatment.

The Vietnamese make masterly salads, and you often find toasted peanuts sprinkled over them to give them extra crunch (and protein too, which is important if you are a vegetarian).

When I'm putting nuts into salads—apart from pine nuts—I sometimes like to complement them with a dash of their oil. However, as I've said elsewhere, nut and seed oils deteriorate very fast, so buy them in small bottles and use them quickly. I keep them in the refrigerator when opened—though some oil purists disapprove of this.

So, match macadamias to macadamia oil, pumpkin seeds to (a few drops only) of beautiful green pumpkin seed oil, hazelnuts with their oil, walnuts with theirs, sesame seeds with a few drops of toasted sesame oil. But, if you don't have the required oil, don't worry—just use good olive oil and the toasted nut (toasted in a dry skillet). And if you haven't yet discovered avocado oil, start today—it's good for salad, and wonderful for cooking.

crisp fried things

I don't know why, but the human palate just loves crispy, crunchy things. Yes, I know celery and apples fall into that category, but add a little bit of oil and perhaps a dash of salt, and suddenly we are devoted to the crispy texture.

vegetable chips

Thinly slice onions, shallots, garlic, pumpkin, or parsnips, using a mandoline or vegetable peeler. Fill a wok or deep-fryer one-third full of peanut oil, or other mild-flavored oil.

Heat the oil to about 380°F or to the manufacturer's recommended temperature. Test using an inexpensive candy thermometer, or drop in a cube of bread—it should turn golden brown in about 30–40 seconds—or a piece of noodle, which should puff up immediately.

Add the sliced vegetables in batches (not too many at a time) and cook on both sides until crisp and golden. Drain on crumpled paper towels. If you want to keep them warm, do so in a low oven.

deep-fried herbs

Herb leaves such as parsley, sage, curry leaves, and others are delicious fried to a crisp, either in a wok or deep-fryer as above, or shallow-fried in a skillet using olive oil or a mixture of butter and oil.

asian crispy things

Asian supermarkets sell interesting crispy things that are wonderful for topping all kinds of dishes. I like Vietnamese fried shallots, onions, or garlic; Asian dried shrimp, which can be used as is, or ground to a powder and toasted some more. Japanese bonito flakes, that are used in making dashi stock, also have good salady uses.

herb and spice oils

You can buy herb oils and chile oils, but I much prefer to make them myself.

basil oil

To make basil oil, put a large handful of basil in a food processor and add at least 1 cup olive oil. Blend, set aside for 30 minutes or overnight in the refrigerator, then strain into a clean bottle. Other herbs, such as parsley, may be used instead.

chile oil

To make chile oil, put a few fresh or dried chiles in a small bottle of oil. Let steep for a few hours or up to 1 day, then taste. If the oil is spicy enough for you, strain out the chiles, return the oil to the bottle and seal. If not, let steep longer, to taste.

leaves

mesclun

Mesclun comes from the same origin as the word "miscellaneous." In Italian, it's *insalata di campo*—little salad of the fields. Choose a combination of leaves—some crisp, some bitter, some peppery, some soft—and sprigs of scented herbs. The perfection of the dressing is what's important. My view is that the oil must be as marvelous as possible and the vinegar as little as possible. I prefer it without mustard or garlic, but please yourself.

Wash the lettuce leaves as necessary and spin dry in a salad spinner. Put in plastic bags or wrap in dry dish towels and chill for at least 30 minutes to crisp. (If washing soft leaves like arugula, do it at the last minute, otherwise they will go mushy—thankfully, my supermarket sells them in bags, already washed and dried.)

If using garlic, put it on a board with a pinch of sea salt and crush thoroughly with the back of a heavy knife (use a garlic crusher if you must, but I think the texture is better this way). Transfer to a salad bowl, add the olive oil, vinegar, mustard, if using, and pepper, then beat with a fork or small whisk. Add extra salt and pepper, to taste.

When ready to serve, add the leaves and, using your hands, turn them gently in the dressing until lightly coated. (I prefer to use my hands, so as not to bruise the leaves and to make sure every one is well coated.) Alternatively, if you have used a large proportion of soft leaves, serve the salad undressed, with the dressing in a small pitcher. The salad can then be dressed by your guests just before eating.

note

A few tablespoons of dressing is plenty for a salad of this size—too much will spoil it. I also prefer the vinegar to be as gentle as possible. (White rice vinegar is my current favorite, but I also like sherry vinegar.)

salad forks

Do you remember the scene in *Pretty Woman* when Hector Elizondo teaches Julia Roberts the proper etiquette for forks? With a place setting of modern flatware, you are expected to use the small fork for salads, but the Victorians had a much more complicated regime. There were special pieces of cutlery for everything. Lettuce knives were never sharp, because you weren't supposed to cut the delicate leaves (they were always torn into bite-size pieces). Salad forks on the other hand, had five tines, the outer ones were always wider, so they wouldn't damage the leaves. You can still buy these pretty forks in antique shops.

your choice of:

crisp leaves, such as romaine hearts

soft leaves, such as oakleaf lettuce

peppery leaves, such as watercress or nasturtium leaves or flowers

bitter leaves, such as dandelion or endive

arugula and wild arugula, if available

soft herb sprigs, such as fennel, parsley, or basil

dressing

1/2 garlic clove (optional)

a pinch of sea salt flakes

6 parts extra virgin olive oil

1 part vinegar, such as cider, white rice, sherry, white wine, or red wine

1 teaspoon Dijon mustard (optional)

freshly ground black pepper

serves 4–6

caesar salad

This is probably the most famous salad in the world and the perfect combination of salty, crispy crunch. It seems to have been around forever, but not so—it was invented by Italian chef Caesar Cardini in Tijuana, Mexico, in 1924. Note that this recipe serves one person—just multiply the ingredients to serve more people.

1 egg, preferably free range and organic

6 smallest leaves of romaine lettuce

1/2 tablespoon freshly squeezed lemon juice, plus 1 lemon cut into wedges, to serve (optional)

2 tablespoons extra virgin olive oil

3–4 canned anchovy fillets, rinsed and drained

Parmesan cheese, at room temperature, shaved into curls with a vegetable peeler

sea salt and freshly ground black pepper

croutons

1 thick slice crusty white bread or challah bread

2 tablespoons oil and/or butter, for cooking

1 garlic clove, crushed

serves 1

To cook the egg, put in a small saucepan and bring to a boil. Reduce the heat and simmer for 4–5 minutes. Remove from the heat and cover with cold water to stop it cooking further. Let cool a little, then peel. Cut into quarters just before serving.

To make the croutons, tear the bread into bite-size chunks, brush with oil or butter, and rub with the garlic. Cook on a preheated stove-top grill pan until crisply golden and barred with brown. Alternatively, follow one of the methods on page 29.

Put the lettuce in a large bowl and sprinkle with salt and pepper, add the lemon juice and toss with your hands. Finally, sprinkle with olive oil and toss again.

Put the croutons in a bowl and put the dressed leaves on top. Add the anchovies, egg, and Parmesan, sprinkle with pepper, and serve with lemon wedges, if using.

notes

• Of course, the croutons were traditionally made of sliced bread cut into cubes, and I love them made this way. Just for a change, however, I've made them freeform, so you get lots of crisp, crunchy edges. Be classic if you prefer.

• Originally, the salad used a one-minute egg—coddled, rather than boiled—so that the egg became part of the dressing. These days, some people are nervous about eggs, so I have done it my favorite way—simmered for 4–5 minutes after the water has come to a boil. The white will be set, but the yolk still soft and creamy.

endive with chorizo

Salads don't have to be complicated. This one is very simple—
shown here as an appetizer, though you can easily increase the
quantities and serve as a side salad with pasta or other dishes.
Belgian endive has a juicy but bitter leaf. Bitter seems to go very
well with a little spice—from Dijon mustard, or from the smoky
paprika flavor of the chorizo. There are different kinds of chorizo
available—the ones you need are the small, whole slightly dried
sausages, about 3½ inches long and perhaps ¾-inch diameter,
sold in strings. The ones with white strings are known as sweet,
the ones with red are spicy (very).

Put the chorizo on a chopping board and slice very thinly with a sharp knife. Heat the olive
oil in a skillet, then add the chorizo slices. Sauté until brown on one side, then turn them
over and brown the other side. They will be quite crisp. Remove from the heat.

Make the vinaigrette in a salad bowl. Cut the root end off the endive, pull the leaves apart,
and add them to the bowl. Toss well, then pile onto 4 salad plates. Add the chorizo, then
sprinkle any of the spicy red oil from the pan over the top (this is the best part).

note

When choosing endive, remember the paler they are, the less bitter they will be—the
bitterness is bleached out by blanching under cover.

variation

Endive is also very good with Blue Cheese Dressing (pages 21, 42).

2 small sweet chorizo sausages
(not the larger chorizo, sold in slices
like salami)

2 tablespoons olive oil

4–6 heads of Belgian endive, pink,
white, or both, as pale as possible

1 recipe Vinaigrette with Dijon
Mustard (page 21)

serves 4

il cicorino con l'aglio
escarole with olive oil

Gabriella, who is the art director of this book, is from Milan, and this is her favorite salad. In Italy, the leaves are sold in supermarkets, ready-shredded in plastic containers. It can be difficult to find this particular variety at some times of the year, or in some areas. It helps if you remember it as one of the firm-leaf varieties of escarole, also known as chicory or endive, according to where you live. It is slightly bitter in taste, so look for something with the same characteristics. *Il cicorino* is the traditional accompaniment to grilled steak—*tagliata*. Remember, Italians taste and add ingredients to their salad dressings as needed, since every oil, every vinegar—even salt—is different.

Remove the hard cicorino stalks, if any, and arrange the leaves one on top of the other on a wooden board. Finely slice them into a "chiffonade."

Put the garlic, salt and vinegar in a small bowl and beat with a fork. Beat in the olive oil. Taste, and add pepper, or extra salt, vinegar or oil, beating as you go.

Put the cicorino in a salad bowl and trickle the dressing over the top. Toss and serve with grilled steak.

note

A chiffonade is a tangle of finely sliced lettuce, usually iceberg. These strong escarole leaves are one of the few other salad leaves you can cut in this way—most leaves are better torn.

8 oz. cicorino (escarole-type bitter leaves)

1 garlic clove, crushed

1 tablespoon red wine vinegar

6 tablespoons extra virgin olive oil

sea salt and freshly ground black pepper

grilled steak, cut into strips, to serve

serves 4

a wedge with blue

My thanks to photographer Peter Cassidy for this perfect idea for iceberg. After sneering at this old-fashioned lettuce for many a long year, I have "found iceberg" again. I think its reputation was ruined by years of shredding, appearing in the nastiest sandwiches, ghastly buffet salads, and general lettuce abuse. It's one of the few lettuces that can be cut, but don't overdo it. Serving it in a wedge is as violent as iceberg handling should be! The blue cheese dressing is one of my favorites. And, amazingly, we've found this dish makes great party fingerfood.

1 firm whole head of iceberg lettuce

blue cheese dressing

4 oz. Gorgonzola dolcellate or other blue cheese, crumbled

1/3 cup extra virgin olive oil

2 tablespoons white wine vinegar

sea salt and freshly ground black pepper

serves 4

To make the dressing, put the crumbled cheese in a bowl. Crush it up as much as you can with a fork. Add 2 tablespoons of the olive oil and mash until creamy, adding the remaining olive oil and the vinegar as you go. If the end result is too thick, beat in a little hot water until the mixture is loose and creamy. Add salt and pepper to taste—take care with the salt, because blue cheese is already quite salty. The dressing will thicken on standing, so you may need to beat it again just before serving.

Remove the outer leaves of the iceberg and trim the stem.

Cut the lettuce into 4–8 wedges, depending on size, and cut out any thick stalk. Put it on a plate, curved side down, like a boat. Trickle the blue cheese dressing over the top.

note

The white juice that comes out of the stalk when you cut it is lettuce milk, an old-fashioned cure for insomnia.

greek horta salad

In Australia, Greek migrants arrived after World War II bearing wonderful fruits and vegetables, olive oil, and a way with herbs that helped to transform our food. I bought a huge bunch of beets, with fresh leaves and purple stems, from my Greek greengrocer in Sydney. This is the recipe he suggested, and it's also good made with spinach, silver beet, or ruby chard. I've included some baby beet wedges too, just because they're pretty (though the recipe then isn't literally *horta*).

Wash the beetroot leaves, then put in a wide saucepan just with the water clinging to the leaves. Bring to a boil, put the lid on tightly, lower the heat, and simmer for a few minutes until the leaves have just wilted. The time will depend on the kind of leaves you've used.

Remove, cool under running water, and drain. Chill until ready to serve, still draining.

When ready to serve. Put in a wide dish and sprinkle with olive oil, then with sea salt and cracked black pepper. Serve with the lemon, which should be squeezed over just before eating.

variation

Add cooked beet wedges to the salad. Wash any earth off the beets, but do not damage them. Leave the roots on. To cook the beets, either boil or roast. The cooking times will vary according to size—test one with a skewer after about 30 minutes.

To boil, put them in a saucepan, cover with cold water, bring to a boil, and simmer until almost tender. Salt the water, then simmer until done. Let cool, then slip off the skins. If small, leave them whole, otherwise cut into halves or wedges.

To roast, rub the beets with olive oil, sprinkle with salt and cook in a preheated oven at 400°F until done. Remove from the oven, let cool, then cut into wedges. I often leave the skins on the roasted version.

a huge handful of beet leaves (or, if unavailable, spinach, Swiss chard, or ruby chard)

a bunch of baby beets, about 6–8 (optional)

¼ cup olive oil

1 lemon, quartered or cut into wedges

sea salt and freshly cracked black pepper

serves 4

vegetables
and fruit

le grand aïoli

This great Provençal salad can be turned into the best al fresco meal of them all. The basis is garlic mayonnaise, served with fresh and blanched vegetables, a splendid whole poached fish, chilled seafood, cold roasted poultry or beef, and lots of crusty bread. This is a meal for lots of guests, however many will fit around your table. Set up outside, perhaps under a tree. Look out at the sunlight, the garden, the pool, the beach—and keep the wine cool and take hours about it.

In the morning, about 2 hours before lunch, prepare the poached fish. Make sure all the scales have been removed and trim the insides. Put the fish in a fish poacher or large baking dish, cover with stock or water, then add the garlic, onion, and herbs. Bring to a boil, put the lid on tightly (or cover the dish with foil), turn off the heat, and let cool.

To prepare the cooked vegetables, bring a large saucepan of water to a boil and have a large bowl of ice and water ready. Add the beans, blanch for about 2 minutes, then, using tongs, remove to a strainer and cool under the tap. Put the beans in the ice water. The method is the same for all the cooked vegetables—you are aiming for parboiled but still crisp. Sugar snaps and asparagus take about 1 minute, carrots 4–5 minutes, according to size, fennel about 3 minutes, depending on size, and onions about 1–2 minutes or until tender. Do not throw away the water between blanchings, because it all adds flavor to each addition. Finally, boil the peas for 1–2 minutes until cooked but not soft, then drain and chill.

When thoroughly chilled, drain all the cooked vegetables, then put each variety in a small bowl. Toss each one in a light vinaigrette to stop them drying out. Add chopped mint to the carrots. Cover with plastic wrap and chill. Prepare all the uncooked vegetables, wash, drain, and trim. Set on platters, cover with plastic wrap, and chill until ready to serve.

Carefully remove the fish from the cold poaching liquid and transfer to a large platter. Remove and discard the skin and dry the platter with paper towels. Put the lemon wedges around the fish. Set the platter and all the vegetables the table and spoon the aïoli into a big bowl. Let your guests help themselves, cut lots of crunchy bread, and serve red and chilled white wines and lots of sparkling water.

1 whole fish, such as salmon

salted fish stock or water, to cover

6 garlic cloves, halved

1 onion, sliced

a bunch of herbs, such as thyme, rosemary, and bay leaves

at least 2 quantities of Aïoli (page 22)

6 lemons, cut into wedges

chilled uncooked vegetables, for example

cherry tomatoes, on the vine

Belgian endive, red or white, leaves separated

scallions

red bell peppers, preferably long ones (Cubanelle), seeded and sliced lengthwise

chilled blanched vegetables, for example

thin green beans

asparagus

sugar snap peas and/or peas

baby carrots

baby fennel

baby onions

baby zucchini, halved lengthwise

serves: an inflatable number of feasters

avocado salad

Avocado is probably my favorite salad ingredient—so creamy and delicious it can really be used as a dressing in itself. My only rule is to scoop out the flesh with a teaspoon into round, rough balls—I see no point in cutting it into wedges, which is difficult to do and never looks tidy. I mix avocado with whatever looks good that day—shrimp, crab, smoked fish, or smoked chicken, all pulled into shreds—top it just with a few herb leaves if they're handy, grind lots of pepper over it, maybe add a squeeze of lemon juice, and eat it without any dressing. Avocado loves salty things, like seafood, smoked food—and bacon. If you have to share it with others, by all means serve it with these salad leaves and a regular dressing.

If using prosciutto, cut the slices into 3–4 pieces. Heat a skillet, brush with 1 tablespoon olive oil, add the prosciutto or bacon, and cook at medium heat, without disturbing the pieces, until crisp on one side. Using tongs, turn the slices over and sauté until crisp and papery but not too brown. Remove and drain on paper towels.

Put the dressing ingredients in a salad bowl and beat with a fork or small whisk. When ready to serve, add the leaves and turn in the dressing, using your hands. Cut the avocados in half and remove the seeds. Using a teaspoon, scoop out balls of avocado into the salad. Toss gently if you like (though this will send the avocado to the bottom of the bowl). Add the crispy prosciutto or bacon and serve.

note

• To test an avocado for ripeness, don't stick your thumb in it. Cradle it in the palm of your hand and squeeze gently. If it just gives to the pressure, it's perfect.

• It's not true that keeping the seed in guacamole or other avocado dish will stop it going brown. However, lime juice, lemon juice, or vinegar will. I prefer to add it to dishes at the very last minute so it has no chance to discolor.

6 very thin slices prosciutto or bacon

1–2 ripe Hass avocados

1 tablespoon olive oil, for sautéing

8 oz. salad leaves—a mixture of soft, crisp, and peppery

dressing

1/3 cup extra virgin olive oil

1 tablespoon cider vinegar or rice vinegar

1 garlic clove, crushed

1 teaspoon Dijon mustard

sea salt and freshly ground black pepper

serves 4

papaya ginger salsa

There are two kinds of salsa—the sauce kind and the salad kind. Both these recipes are salads, delicious served with main dishes, in tortillas, or as a bed for other ingredients as an appetizer. This one is terrific with fish and seafood.

Peel the peppers with a vegetable peeler, then cut off the tops and bottoms, scoop out the seeds and membranes, and cut the flesh down one side. Open it out into a long rectangle. Cut the rectangle into squares, about 1/2 inch.

Squeeze the grated ginger through a garlic press into a serving bowl. Add the lime juice, and sugar, salt, and pepper to taste. Beat with a fork, then add the peppers and chile. Toss gently, then add the papaya, cilantro, and lime zest and toss gently so as not to break up the papaya. Top with the lime wedges and serve.

1 red bell pepper

1 yellow bell pepper

1 large red chile, seeded and chopped

2 inches fresh ginger, peeled and grated

finely grated zest and juice of 2 unwaxed limes, plus lime wedges, to serve

1 teaspoon sugar, or to taste (optional)

1 ripe papaya, peeled, seeded, and cubed

a large handful of cilantro

sea salt and freshly ground black pepper

serves 4

avocado salsa

Avocado is very good with peppery ingredients as well as salty. I think this salsa is well suited to chicken dishes or even on its own, piled onto crusty bread.

2 very small red onions

4 scallions with large bulbs

2 tablespoons coarsely chopped fresh parsley

2 tablespoons coarsely chopped fresh mint

1 jalapeño or serrano chile, seeded and very finely chopped

2 ripe Hass avocados, halved and seeds removed

lime dressing

freshly squeezed juice of 2 limes

2 tablespoons olive oil

sea salt and freshly ground black pepper

serves 4

Cut the onions in half lengthwise (discard the green stalk on the scallions). Peel off the outside layer, then cut into feathery petals lengthwise through the root. Slice the scallions diagonally.

Mix the dressing ingredients in a large bowl. Add the onions, parsley, mint, and chile and toss lightly in the dressing. Using a teaspoon, scoop the avocado into the bowl and stir very gently to cover with the dressing, then serve.

waldorf salad

When I first made this salad, the apples were unpeeled and cut into chunks, so eating it became rather hard work. I found this more elegant, Edwardian version in an old cookbook and have combined the two. It's good with grills—and suits pork very well, since pork and apples were made for each other. Make it with ripe Granny Smiths so they won't be too tart, or choose crisp red apples instead. The dressing is also old-fashioned, but though it seems unusual now, it's delicious. Use mayonnaise if you prefer.

To prepare the salad, cut a few slices of apple with skin for decoration, then peel and core the remainder and cut into matchstick strips, using a mandoline. Toss them in the lemon juice to stop them turning brown. Finely slice the celery, put in a bowl, add the apples, and walnuts, then spoon the sauce over the top.

note

Mayonnaise is one of the classic dressings for Waldorf, but I must admit I prefer the Lemon Cream Dressing on page 63. It sounds unlikely, but it is incredibly light.

3–4 Granny Smith apples

freshly squeezed juice of 1 lemon

2 celery stalks, thinly sliced

4 oz. walnut pieces or pecans, coarsely chopped, about 1 cup

½ cup Classic Mayonnaise (page 22) or Lemon Cream Dressing (page 63)

serves 4

fennel and mint salad

I had to include this simple salad, invented on a lovely autumn weekend staying with friends at their farmhouse in Umbria.

4 small heads of fennel, trimmed and quartered lengthwise

2 small flat Italian onions (*cipolline*), or ½ mild red onion

a handful of parsley, snipped

a handful of mint, torn

sea salt and freshly ground black pepper

1 recipe Italian Dressing, made with red wine vinegar (page 21)

serves 4

Finely slice the fennel and put in a bowl. If using flat Italian onions, cut them in half put the 2 halves together. Finely slice them into half-moons. If using other onions, finely slice and chop. If they are very peppery, put them in a colander and pour boiling water over them, then drain. Add to the salad.

Sprinkle the parsley and mint over the salad and toss well. Add the Italian dressing, toss well, taste, and add more of the vinaigrette ingredients if necessary. Serve as part of an antipasti or lunch.

red salad with beets, red cabbage, and harissa dressing

I devised this recipe one summer's day when friends were coming over for a barbecue party. They were going to have a regular red coleslaw, but I had a few small beets that day, and the food stylist in me couldn't resist the color combination. Crushing the cabbage and vinegar together with your hands has a miraculous effect on the cabbage, breaking its fibers and releasing its juices. Delicious.

6–8 small beets

2–4 small whole heads of garlic

1 small red cabbage

2 tablespoons white wine vinegar, cider vinegar, or lemon juice

2 red onions or 6 scallions

1 tablespoon umeboshi plum vinegar (page 14), or to taste (optional)

olive oil, for brushing

sea salt and freshly ground black pepper

2 medium red chiles, finely sliced (optional), to serve

harissa dressing

½ cup cold-pressed extra virgin olive oil

1 tablespoon harissa paste or 1 teaspoon chile oil

serves 4–6

Leave the beets whole and unpeeled. Cut the top off each garlic—you will be able to see all the cloves. Put the beets and garlic in a small baking dish, add olive oil, and turn to coat on all sides, then sprinkle with salt and pepper. Put more oil in the garlic. Roast in a preheated oven at 400°F for about 30–45 minutes or until the beets and garlic are tender (you may have to remove the beets early). Baste several times during cooking, spooning the oil into the garlic. When cooked, remove from the oven and cut the beets into 4 wedges (peel them or not, as you like).

About 15 minutes before the beets are cooked, cut the cabbage in quarters and remove the white cores. Cut the quarters into fine slices and put in a bowl. Sprinkle with vinegar and turn and mash the cabbage with your hands so the fibers break down a little and absorb it.

Cut the red onions into fine wedges, put in a bowl, and cover with boiling water. Drain just before using. If using scallions, just chop them coarsely, white and green.

When ready to serve, pop the roasted pulp out of 4 garlic cloves and put in a serving bowl. Add the olive oil and harissa and beat with a fork. Drain the onions, pat dry with paper towels, then add to the bowl. Sprinkle with umeboshi plum vinegar, if using. Add the cabbage and beets and toss gently.

Taste and adjust the seasoning with salt and pepper, and top with the chiles, if using. Put the heads of garlic beside for people to press out the delicious flesh themselves.

spicy coleslaw

I'm not a fan of regular coleslaw, but I love the Indian way with salads. Their vegetables are glorious—super-organic, not irrigated into a complete lack of flavor—and their varieties are much more interesting than factory-farmed versions. I particularly love their huge, bright red winter carrots, which I hope to find in a farmers' market here soon.

Halve the onions lengthwise, then slice into fine wedges, to make petals. Slice the tomatoes, removing any white core, and finely slice the carrot diagonally or into matchsticks. Halve the cucumbers lengthwise, then slice diagonally. Put all the vegetables on a serving plate, cover, and chill.

Put the lemon juice, salt, pepper, and sugar in a bowl, stir, and chill. When ready to serve, sprinkle the vegetables with the dressing, add the mint, and serve.

variation

Indians don't use olive oil, but if you prefer, dress this salad with regular vinaigrette.

2 red onions

2 ripe tomatoes, such as plum

1 carrot

2 Kirby cucumbers, or about 8 inches regular cucumber

1/2 Savoy cabbage, halved, cored, and finely sliced

freshly squeezed juice of 1 lemon or 2 key limes

sea salt and freshly ground black pepper

a pinch of sugar

a small bunch of mint, chopped, plus a few leaves, to serve

serves 4

classic coleslaw

If I didn't include a regular coleslaw, my sister would never forgive me. This is the salad she has forced me to make every Christmas from the beginning of time. Since she acquired a food processor, all the slicing and grating hasn't been such an onerous task, but I still secretly prefer the vegetables to be hand-sliced.

1 cup Classic Mayonnaise (page 22)

1/2 cup Vinaigrette (page 20), or to taste

1 large white cabbage, thinly sliced

1 carrot, grated

1 red bell pepper, peeled, seeded, and chopped (optional)

a handful of parsley and chives, coarsely chopped

1 teaspoon caraway seeds (optional)

sea salt and freshly ground black pepper

variation dressing
Lemon Cream Dressing (page 63)

serves 8

To make the dressing, put the mayonnaise in a small bowl, add half the vinaigrette, and beat well. Taste, then add more vinaigrette, 1 tablespoon at a time, until the taste and creaminess is right. The amount will depend on the flavor of the original dressings. Set aside.

Put all the vegetables in a bowl and mix well. Add half the dressing and toss to coat. Add more dressing until the texture pleases you (in our family we don't like too much dressing). Season to taste with caraway seeds, if using, then salt and pepper, then cover and chill until needed. This will develop the flavors. Let return to room temperature for a few minutes, stir in the parsley and chives, then serve.

fruit and vegetables
with yogurt dressing

Indian salads or raitas almost always include yogurt as the main element of the dressing, with toasted spices, called the "tempering," as the flavor note. You can use almost any crisp fruit or vegetable in this salad—vary the ingredients according to what's in season. The keynotes are crisp, sweet, and spicy.

To make the dressing, put the ajwain, mustard seeds, and red pepper flakes in a dry skillet and toast over medium heat until aromatic. Transfer to a small bowl and let cool. Add the salt and sugar, then grate the ginger and squeeze the gratings into the bowl. Stir in the yogurt and set aside.

Put the cashews in the same pan and toast over medium heat until golden. Do not let burn. Remove from the heat, transfer to a small bowl, and let cool. When cool, chop coarsely.

Put the lettuce wedges on a plate, add the pomelo pieces, if using, grapes, radishes, cucumber, and ginger. Spoon over the dressing—sparingly—don't drown it. Then sprinkle with the cashews, coconut, and cilantro, if using.

note

I have used a few sprigs of methi in the photograph. They are the leaves of the fenugreek plant—the seeds are the spice that makes curry powder smell of curry. The leaves are used as a green vegetable in Indian cooking, but when I can get them, I also like just a few fresh sprigs in salads. They give a very faint and fascinating scent of curry to the salad. They are difficult to find, but interesting.

¼ cup cashews

4 small crisp lettuces, cut into wedges or torn into pieces

6 segments pomelo or grapefruit (preferably pink), membranes removed, segments pulled into 2–3 pieces (optional)

12 large red or white grapes, or both, halved lengthwise and seeded

6 red radishes, finely sliced on a mandoline

1 Kirby cucumber, halved lengthwise, seeded and finely sliced on a mandoline

1 inch fresh ginger, peeled and finely sliced into thin slivers on a mandoline (julienne blade)

¼ cup unsweetened flaked coconut, soaked in water if dried (optional)

sprigs of cilantro (optional)

yogurt dressing

a pinch of lovage (ajwain) seeds (optional)

1 teaspoon mustard seeds

a pinch of hot red pepper flakes

½ teaspoon salt

½ teaspoon sugar

1 inch fresh ginger, peeled

1 cup plain yogurt

serves 4

classic potato salad

I have always been mystified by the dressing on my mother's potato salad, which she made in quantity for local farmers' meetings. In those days, the only oils for cooking were bacon fat and butter. So what did she use? My sister came to the rescue …

Put the potatoes in a large saucepan, cover with cold water, add a large pinch of salt, and bring to a boil over medium heat. Reduce the heat immediately and simmer gently until done (potatoes should always be cooked gently)—they should be cooked but still firm.

Drain. As soon as they are cool enough to touch, peel them—hold them in a dry cloth and pull off the skins with the back of a dinner knife. Slice them thickly and put in a salad bowl. Season with plenty of salt and pepper, then add the onions.

To make the dressing, put the salt, pepper, and lemon juice in a bowl, stir to dissolve the salt, then gradually pour in the cream, stirring constantly. This dressing must be used immediately. Alternatively, use the traditional dressing ingredients, mixed well.

While still warm, pour the dressing over the potatoes and stir carefully, so that each piece is coated with the dressing. Gently fold in the boiled eggs. Top with the herbs and spring onions and serve. Potato salad is nicer when cool, not chilled, so if you've had to refrigerate it, let it return to room temperature first.

2 lb. potatoes, such as Yukon Gold, unpeeled
2 mild onions, finely sliced into rings
6 hard-cooked eggs, chopped
salt and freshly ground white pepper

lemon cream dressing
freshly squeezed juice of 1 lemon
1 cup heavy cream
sea salt and white pepper

traditional dressing (optional)
1 recipe Classic Mayonnaise (page 22)
1/2 cup milk

to serve
a large bunch of parsley, chopped
a small bunch of mint, chopped
a handful of chives, snipped
4 spring onions, thinly sliced

serves 6

indian potato salad

On the other hand, the Indian variety of this comforting salad is spicy, crunchy, and wonderfully interesting. Add extra lime juice to taste. The spice mixes may be changed to suit your taste.

Heat the oil in a large skillet, add the mustard and cumin seeds, cinnamon, chile, and cardamom. Stir-fry until aromatic, then stir in the turmeric. Add the potatoes, salt, and pepper and cook for about 2 minutes. Add 1 cup water and boil until the liquid has evaporated and the potatoes are tender—add more water if necessary.

Sprinkle half the chopped onions over the top and add the cilantro. Heat the oil in a small skillet, add the remaining onion and the garlic, and sauté until golden. Pour over the potatoes and toss to coat. Top with the torn cilantro and serve.

1/4 cup peanut oil or ghee
1 tablespoon mustard seeds
1/2 tablespoon cumin seeds
1/2 cinnamon stick, crushed
1 dried red chile, crushed
6 cardamom pods, crushed
1 teaspoon turmeric
1 lb. potatoes, cut into chunks
2 red onions, chopped
1/4 cup peanut oil or ghee
1 garlic clove, crushed
a handful of cilantro, torn
salt and freshly ground black pepper

serves 4

big greek salad

Greek salads are so much part of the easy, Mediterranean style of eating—a bit of crisp, a bit of fiery, a few baby herbs, some vinegary olives (and Greece produces some of the best), and salty anchovies. I used to live in Melbourne, the second biggest Greek city in the world. I remember marvelous lunches where we snacked on a communal salad like this one as we waited for the best efforts of chefs from Kalymnos, where many Australian Greek families came from. I love proper Kalamata olives, but unpitted, because they have more flavor—warn your guests in case they're not expecting them.

1 head iceberg lettuce, quartered and torn apart

about 8 oz. feta cheese, crumbled into big pieces, or cut into cubes

6 oz. Kalamata olives, about 1 cup

2 red onions, halved, then sliced into petals

2 Kirby cucumbers, halved lengthwise, then thinly sliced diagonally

4 big ripe red tomatoes, cut into chunks

8 anchovies, or to taste

a few sprigs of oregano, torn

a few sprigs of mint, torn

greek dressing

⅓ cup extra virgin olive oil, preferably Greek

2 tablespoons freshly squeezed lemon juice

sea salt and freshly ground black pepper

serves 4

Put the lettuce in a large bowl. Add the cheese, olives, onions, cucumbers, and tomatoes.

To make the dressing, put the olive oil, lemon juice, salt, and pepper in a bowl, beat with a fork, then pour over the salad. You can also sprinkle them onto the salad separately.

Top with the anchovies, oregano, and mint, and serve.

notes

• Iceberg is one of the few lettuces than can bear to be sliced. Slice it if you wish, but I like big chunky bits.

• My favorite things in a Greek salad are the salted anchovies, so I have extra. Greek markets sell them in big cans—wheels of whole fish, arranged nose to tail. You rinse and fillet them yourself. However, if you don't have a Greek market, use canned.

italian grilled pepper salad

A beautiful, delicious, simple salad based on the classic Insalata Caprese. If you find yourself without the most important ingredient for this salad (the very best, ripest, most flavorful tomatoes), peppers are a great solution. This salad comes from my cousin, who lives outside Naples—we have driven along country roads, buying mozzarella from the farmers and collecting arugula from the roadside verges (and peppers and tomatoes grown in local gardens).

Put the whole peppers under a hot broiler, on a grill, or over the flame of a gas stove. Cook on all sides until charred. Remove from the heat, transfer to a saucepan, and put on the lid (this will help steam off the skins). When cool, drain the juices into a small bowl.

Scrape off and discard the charred skins. Cut the peppers in half lengthwise and scrape out and discard the seeds and membranes, adding any juices to the bowl.

To make the dressing, put 2 tablespoons of the juices in another bowl with the olive oil. Beat with a fork. Add salt and pepper to taste, and extra pepper juice if you like. (Keep any extra juice for another use.)

When ready to assemble the salad, tear the mozzarellas apart into big shreds—about 4 pieces each—and put on 4 chilled plates. Add a handful of arugula and 2 pepper halves to each plate. Sprinkle with the olive oil, then add a few drops of balsamic, if using, to each serving. Sprinkle with sea salt flakes and cracked pepper and serve.

notes

• Please don't slather the balsamic over the salad. Use it as a seasoning, not a dressing.

• The best mozzarella is made from buffalo milk and comes from Campania around Naples. If you don't have any buffaloes handy, any good-quality fresh mozzarella may be used. Just don't cut it—tear it apart, so it separates along its natural grain.

• There are different kinds of arugula. In my garden, I have four—in my refrigerator, I have two. Supermarkets sell the round-leafed seedling kind, and sometimes also the variety with jagged leaves. Around Naples it does grow wild along country roads, where the locals gather it in season. You can try growing a few seeds in a window box or flowerpot—keep sowing and keep picking.

4 large red bell peppers or Cubanelle

2 mozzarella cheeses, preferably *mozzarella di bufala*, about 8 oz.

4 handfuls of arugula, torn

¼ cup best-quality, cold-pressed extra virgin olive oil

balsamic vinegar (optional)

sea salt and freshly ground black pepper

serves 4

tuscan panzanella

There are as many variations of this Tuscan bread salad as there are cooks—some old recipes don't even include tomatoes. The trick is to let the flavors blend well without the bread disintegrating into a mush. Always use the ripest, reddest, most flavorful tomatoes you can find—Brandywine is a favorite variety, or you could use one of the other full-flavored heirloom varieties, such as Black Russian or Green Zebra, or at least an Italian plum tomato.

6 very ripe tomatoes

2 garlic cloves, sliced into slivers

4 thick slices day-old bread, preferably Italian-style, such as pugliese or ciabatta

about 4 inches cucumber, halved, seeded, and thinly sliced diagonally

1 red onion, chopped

1 tablespoon chopped fresh flat-leaf parsley

1/2–3/4 cup extra virgin olive oil

2 tablespoons white wine vinegar, cider vinegar or sherry vinegar

a bunch of basil, leaves torn

12 caperberries or 1/4 cup capers packed in brine, rinsed and drained

1 teaspoon balsamic vinegar (optional)

sea salt and freshly ground black pepper

serves 4

Cut the tomatoes in half, spike with slivers of garlic, and roast in a preheated oven at 350°F for about 1 hour, or until wilted and some of the moisture has evaporated.

Meanwhile, put the bread on an oiled stove-top grill pan and cook until lightly toasted and barred with grill marks on both sides. Tear or cut the toast into pieces and put in a salad bowl. Sprinkle with a little water until damp.

Add the tomatoes, cucumber, onion, parsley, salt, and pepper. Sprinkle with the olive oil and cider or sherry vinegar, toss well, then set aside for about 1 hour to develop the flavors.

Add the basil leaves and caperberries or capers and serve sprinkled with a few drops of balsamic vinegar, if using.

green vegetable salad
with hazelnut dressing

Green vegetables, like peas, beans, zucchini, asparagus, and their kin, are favorites of mine. I mix them to serve as an accompaniment to hot dishes, but they are equally good as a cold salad. They live well together with the milder members of the onion family—pearl onions, baby scallions, or red onion. An ordinary vinaigrette will do as well, but I like nut oils such as macadamia, walnut, and hazelnut, and they must be mixed with olive oil.

Microwave the asparagus tips, beans, zucchini, sugar snaps, and green peas separately on HIGH for 2 minutes each, then transfer immediately to a bowl of ice cubes and water. This stops them cooking and sets the color. Alternatively, bring a large saucepan of water to a boil, then add each vegetable and blanch until just tender, but still *al dente*. Keep the peas until the end, and drain well before chilling.

To make the dressing, put the olive oil, vinegar, mustard, salt, and pepper in a salad bowl and beat well with a fork or small whisk to form an emulsion. Put in a bowl, add the drained vegetables, one kind at a time, and toss until lightly coated. Arrange the asparagus, beans, zucchini, and scallions on a serving platter or 4 rectangular salad plates. Add the sugar snaps and green peas, then sprinkle with hazelnut oil, toasted hazelnuts, sea salt flakes, and cracked black pepper. Shave fresh Parmesan over the top and serve.

notes

• Nut oils and nuts become rancid very quickly, so buy them in small quantities. Use them quickly, keep them sealed, and store in the refrigerator, returning to room temperature for serving. Seed oils, such as pumpkin seed or sesame seeds, will suffer the same fate, so do the same with them.

• Green vegetables are one category of foods that perform well in the microwave, which is, after all, just a kind of steaming.

about 12 small asparagus tips·

a handful of thin green beans (untrimmed)

4 baby zucchini, cut into thirds lengthwise (optional)

4 oz. sugar snap peas

4 oz. shelled green peas, about 1 cup

4–6 very thin scallions

sea salt flakes and freshly cracked black pepper

fresh Parmesan cheese, to serve

hazelnut oil dressing

6 parts extra virgin olive oil

1 part Japanese rice vinegar or white wine vinegar

1/2 teaspoon Dijon mustard

hazelnut oil

3 oz. hazelnuts, pan-toasted in a dry skillet, then lightly crushed into halves or big pieces, about 1/2 cup

a little sea salt and freshly cracked black pepper

serves 4

carrot salad
with cilantro curd

I always buy organically grown carrots, and try to find them with their leaves on. Although you can't eat carrot leaves, they are a good indication of how fresh the roots are. A wilted leaf is an old root. This recipe uses mustard oil, which may be new to you. It is available in Asian grocers, but if you can't find it, use another oil, but not olive. Mustard oil is related to the oil made from oilseed rape, the plant that turns our countryside into a blanket of violently bright yellow. It is used in highly refined form to make oils such as vegetable oil or canola. In fact, like most oils, it tastes better and is better for you when cold pressed—you do all the heating yourself in your own skillet. Curd is another word for yogurt.

1½ cups plain yogurt

3 medium carrots, with leaves if possible, trimmed and peeled

2 tablespoons mustard oil or safflower oil

1 tablespoon mustard seeds

1 medium green chile, seeded (optional) and finely sliced

2 tablespoons chopped cilantro and a few sprigs of fresh cilantro

2 sprigs of curry leaves (optional)

sea salt and freshly ground black pepper

serves 4

Put the yogurt in a fine strainer and let drain over a bowl while you prepare the salad.

Using a mandoline or vegetable peeler, cut the peeled carrots into long ribbons. Bring a saucepan of lightly salted water to a boil, add the carrots, return to a boil, and simmer for 2 minutes until limp but not soft. Drain, and rinse under cold running water.

Transfer to a serving bowl, curling the ribbons casually to leave space between them.

Put the oil in a small saucepan or skillet, heat well, then add the mustard seeds, chile, and curry leaves, if using. Sauté until the mustard seeds start to hop out of the pan (a little like popcorn), then pour the mixture over the carrots and let cool.

Put the yogurt in a bowl and whip with electric beaters. Stir in the chopped cilantro and spoon into a small serving bowl. Serve the 2 bowls together, topped with a few sprigs of cilantro. To eat, take a share of the carrots and top with a spoonful of curds.

japanese cucumber salads

Japanese salads, like many Japanese dishes, are wonderfully elegant, often constructed as small towers in tiny bowls. They are usually simple affairs, with just a few elements, perfectly balanced. I love the Japanese way of preparing cucumbers—you sprinkle salt over a work surface, put the whole, unpeeled cucumber on top and roll it hard in the salt. Cut it in half lengthwise, scrape out the seeds, and slice it thinly (a nifty little Japanese mandoline will do this perfectly for you). Rub the slices with salt, wash, drain, and sprinkle with vinegar. It is a preparation method used in many cuisines and worth using in other dishes.

cucumber salad with ginger and seaweed

Prepare the cucumbers as described above, then put in a bowl, sprinkle with 1 teaspoon salt, and rub lightly with your fingers. Wash, drain, and sprinkle with a few drops of vinegar

Put the wakame in a bowl and cover with water. Cut out and discard any hard parts. Drain, then pour boiling water over the top, drain again and cut into 1-inch lengths. Put in a colander, sprinkle with a few drops of vinegar, and set aside while you prepare the dressing.

Put the dressing, cucumber, wakame, and shrimp in a bowl and mix gently. Serve in small bowls with shreds of ginger on top.

crab and cucumber salad

Put the crab in a bowl, remove and discard any stray bits of shell, then sprinkle it with the vinegar and set aside.

Prepare the cucumbers as in the previous recipe—put salt on a cutting board and roll the cucumbers over the top. Cut in half lengthwise, then slice thinly, using a mandoline, if you have one. Put in a strainer, sprinkle with salt, and let drain for 30 minutes. Rinse with water, transfer to a dry cloth, and squeeze out the liquid.

To serve, put a pile of cucumber in a tiny Japanese bowl, with a pile of crabmeat beside or on top, then sprinkle with the dressing and serve.

**cucumber salad
with ginger and seaweed**

2 Kirby cucumbers

1 teaspoon salt

rice vinegar (see method)

3 oz. wakame seaweed

1 recipe Sambai-zu Dressing (page 26)

2–3 freshly cooked medium-to-large shrimp, peeled and thinly sliced crosswise

2 inches fresh ginger, peeled and sliced into fine shreds

crab salad

8 oz. crabmeat, about 1 1/2 cups

1/2 teaspoon rice vinegar

2 Kirby cucumbers

sea salt

1 recipe Kimi-zu Dressing (page 26)

serves 4

nepali radish salad

The vegetable markets of Kathmandu are a riot of color and, at least in the warm months, full of produce of extraordinary quality. The markets run at night too—I remember stumbling in the dark past shrines a thousand years old and women sitting beside lamps selling produce from their gardens. In Nepal, the radish is the white Asian kind, and it is usually blanched first. I added some red radishes to the dish to give some crunchy, peppery contrast.

Peel the daikon and cut into 2-inch pieces, then cut the pieces into thick batons about ½-inch square. Bring a saucepan of lightly salted water to a boil, add the daikon pieces, and blanch for 3–4 minutes. Drain, dip in cold water, then drain and pat dry with paper towels. To prepare the red radishes, slice them finely on a mandoline or cut into wedges.

Put the sesame seeds and mustard seeds in a dry skillet and toast until they start to bounce. Stir in the turmeric, but do not let the seeds burn. Using a mortar and pestle, crush the spices together, then add the salt, pepper, lemon juice, and oil and crush again. You can also use a small blender or spice grinder.

Put the mixture in a bowl, add the blanched daikon, and toss gently until coated with the dressing. Add the red radishes and serve. This is good with other Indian dishes and rice.

notes

• I use a big stone mortar and pestle from Thailand to grind spices. Buy them from Asian markets, where they are relatively inexpensive. I also have a small coffee grinder that I use only for spices.

• This dressing is also good with other vegetables, such as new potatoes dressed with mint, chunks of blanched zucchini, or fresh endomame with chopped chile and a handful of crushed peanuts.

• One of the best ways of serving radishes comes from France—trim them, provide small dishes of butter and sea salt, and let your guests dip and crunch, a method that harks back to the original Roman idea of a salad.

½ daikon (Japanese white radish)
a bunch of red radishes, well washed
sea salt, to taste

sesame mustard dressing

¼ cup white sesame seeds

1 tablespoon mustard seeds

a pinch of turmeric

1 tablespoon freshly squeezed lemon juice

1 tablespoon mustard oil or peanut oil

sea salt and freshly ground black pepper, to taste

serves 4

indonesian gado gado

This is a terrific salad for a large party, and can be adapted for vegetarians if you leave out the shrimp. The original has all the ingredients lined up like soldiers, so you can take your pick of them. I think it's much nicer all higgledy-piggledy so the flavors have a chance to infuse. You can add and subtract ingredients according to what you have on hand and your own preferences.

To make the sauce, toast the peanuts in a dry skillet, transfer to a dish towel, and rub off the skins. When the nuts are cool, transfer to a blender and grind to a coarse meal. Add the chiles, onion, garlic, salt, sugar, and coconut milk. Blend well, then transfer to a saucepan and cook until thickened. Set aside—the sauce will thicken further as it cools. When ready to serve, thin with water to the consistency of light cream.

Bring a large saucepan of salted water to a boil and add the beans. Cook until *al dente*, about 1 minute, then remove to a strainer set over a bowl. Run cold water over them. When cool, transfer to a bowl of ice water. Just before serving, drain again and let dry in the colander.

Peel the bell pepper with a vegetable peeler. Cut off the top and bottom and remove the membranes, open out, and slice thinly.

Put 2 tablespoons of the oil in a skillet, dip the tofu in flour, then add to the skillet and sauté until brown on all sides. Drain and slice thickly.

To cook the shrimp crackers, fill a wok or saucepan two-thirds full of oil and heat until a piece of noodle will puff up immediately. Add the crackers, crowding them so they curl up. After about 3 seconds they should be puffed and airy. Remove and drain on paper towels.

Reheat the oil, add the onion rings, and sauté until crisp and golden. Remove and drain on paper towels.

Arrange all the ingredients on a large serving platter, drizzle with the peanut sauce, top with the onions and shrimp crackers, sprinkle with salt, and serve.

a large handful of green beans, trimmed and halved

1 red or orange bell pepper

1 lb. firm tofu, drained and cut into 2 cakes, about the size of a deck of cards

flour, for dusting

1/2 package shrimp crackers*

2 red onions, sliced

a large handful of bean sprouts, rinsed, drained, and trimmed

1 romaine lettuce heart

6 inches daikon (Japanese white radish), peeled and cut into matchsticks

2 Kirby cucumbers, sliced

2 small hard-cooked eggs, quartered (cook so that the yolks are only just set, page 36)

sea salt

peanut oil, for cooking

peanut sauce

8 oz. shelled raw peanuts, about 1 1/2 cups

2 bird chiles, halved, seeded, and chopped

1 onion, finely chopped

1 garlic clove, crushed

1 teaspoon salt

2 teaspoons brown sugar

1/2 cup canned coconut milk

serves 4

Shrimp crackers are sold in Asian stores in huge packages, but they last well. Keep the package and serve shrimp crackers instead of chips at your next party.

tomato salads

Tomato salads appear in infinite variety. My own favorite is a simple farmer's salad from my childhood. Good, ripe, sliced tomatoes, sprinkled with vinegar, salt, and pepper. No oil. The salt brings out the tomato juices, which help form the dressing. We grew our own then, and the flavor was incomparable. I have put optional sugar in this first recipe to make up for the fact that, as everyone knows, tomatoes don't taste the way they used to! Heirloom varieties, like the Green Zebra shown, Black Russian, or Brandywine, do have that old-fashioned flavor, so look out for them in farmers' markets.

tomato farmer's salad

Put the tomatoes on a plate or in a bowl. Sprinkle with vinegar, salt, and pepper and set aside for a few minutes until ready to serve. Taste, and add a pinch of sugar, if using.

tomato and onion salad

Cut 1 red onion in half lengthwise, then slice it finely, separate the half-rings, and put in the bowl before the tomatoes. Alternatively, use 6 scallions, thinly sliced diagonally. Proceed as in the previous recipe. Turn gently before serving.

tomato salad with dijon vinaigrette and herbs

Prepare the tomatoes as in the first recipe, then sprinkle with Dijon vinaigrette and turn gently with 2 forks so as not to break up the tomatoes. Sprinkle with herbs, then serve.

moroccan-style tomatoes with preserved lemon and harissa vinaigrette (opposite)

To prepare the preserved lemons, cut them in quarters, scrape out and discard the flesh, and cut the skin into strips. Cut the tomatoes into wedges and put them in a bowl with the lemon strips and scallions. Mix gently, then toss in the mint. Set aside for a few minutes for the flavors to develop, then serve with mint leaves on top.

note

Preserved lemons are available in North African and French gourmet stores. If unavailable, substitute the freshly grated zest of 2 unwaxed lemons.

---

4 large, ripe tomatoes (1 per person), sliced, or 1 lb. mixed red and yellow cherry tomatoes, halved

tomato farmer's salad

3–4 tablespoons white wine vinegar

sea salt and freshly ground black pepper

sugar, to taste (optional)

tomato and onion salad

1 red onion or 6 scallions

tomato salad with dijon vinaigrette and herbs

1 recipe Dijon Vinaigrette (pages 21, 83)

a handful of fresh herbs, such as torn basil leaves, snipped chives, or crushed thyme leaves

moroccan-style tomato salad with preserved lemon and harissa vinaigrette

1–2 preserved lemons

2 scallions, chopped

1 recipe Harissa Vinaigrette (page 21)

1 tablespoon chopped fresh mint, plus a handful of leaves, to serve

serves 4

quick chickpea salad

Chickpeas are the basis of some of my favorite lunchtime salads and vegetable entrée accompaniments. Like all dried legumes, they drink up flavors, but unlike some, chickpeas can be relied upon not to fall apart. They're great for picnics and other make-ahead occasions. You can part-prepare them, so the dressing soaks into the chickpeas, then add the fresh ingredients just before serving.

Put the dressing ingredients in a bowl and beat with a fork. Add the chickpeas, artichoke hearts, and semi-dried tomatoes, if using, and toss in the dressing. Cover and chill for up to 4 hours.

When ready to serve, add the cherry tomatoes, scallions, basil, chives, and parsley. Stir gently, then sprinkle with the shaved Parmesan and pepper.

note

Use partially sun-dried tomatoes, sometimes called sun-blushed, which are sold in Italian gourmet stores.

variations

• You can add any number of other ingredients, including olives, prosciutto, salami, or chorizo, canned or grilled fresh tuna, other vegetables, lettuces, or herbs, or your favorite spices.

• Instead of Dijon dressing, dress with Basil Oil (page 30) or other herb oil. A few drops of chile oil in the dressing instead of the mustard give a different kind of fire.

2 cups cooked or canned chickpeas, rinsed and drained (2 cans, 15 oz. each)

4 marinated artichoke hearts

4 large semi-dried tomatoes (optional)

8 oz. very ripe cherry tomatoes, halved

8 scallions, sliced diagonally

a handful of basil, torn

a small bunch of chives, snipped

leaves from 4 sprigs of flat-leaf parsley, chopped

2 oz. fresh Parmesan cheese, shaved

1 tablespoon black pepper, cracked with a mortar and pestle

dijon dressing

1/3 cup extra virgin olive oil

1 tablespoon freshly squeezed lemon juice or sherry vinegar

1 teaspoon Dijon mustard

1 small garlic clove, crushed

sea salt and freshly ground black pepper

serves 4

italian lentil salad

My favorite lentils are the tiny black French Puy lentils or the big Indian yellow channa dhaal. Other green or brown lentils are also good, though I draw the line at the red ones, toorvar dhaal. I think they turn into an unattractive pink mush. You don't need to soak lentils before cooking and, like beans, don't salt them until towards the end. You can also add aromatics such as onion, herbs, garlic, or cinnamon stick to the cooking water. As a slothful cook, however, one of my favorite late-night quick snacks is this salad using canned Italian lentils, which are a pretty maroon color.

2 cups cooked or canned lentils, rinsed and drained, about 15 oz. (if using dried lentils, measure a heaping 1 cup before cooking)

4 preserved baby artichokes, preferably grilled, quartered

1 red onion, halved lengthwise and cut into thin slivered wedges

6 oz. feta cheese, cut into cubes or crumbled into big pieces

a handful of mixed fresh herbs, such as parsley, basil, or marjoram, coarsely chopped, or snipped chives, to serve

italian dressing

a pinch of sea salt (taste the lentils first in case they're already salty)

1 tablespoon cider vinegar

¼ cup extra virgin olive oil

freshly ground black pepper

serves 4

Put the lentils in a bowl, add the pinch of salt (omit if using other salty ingredients, such as feta cheese or anchovies), then the vinegar, oil, and pepper.

Add the artichokes, onion, and feta cheese, then toss gently. Add salt and pepper to taste, then serve, sprinkled with herbs.

variations

• Lentils with cherry tomatoes, black olives, chopped red onions, and crushed garlic, dressed with red wine vinegar vinaigrette. Add a few anchovies (optional).

• Bocconcini or mozzarella cheese, torn into long shreds, with plum tomatoes, scallions, and basil. Add a sprinkle of balsamic vinegar before serving.

• Big ripe tomatoes, seeded but with juices reserved, chopped into big pieces, mixed with preserved lemon peel or *mostarda di frutta* (from an Italian gourmet store), with 1 tablespoon harissa paste added to the dressing.

• Shredded roasted chicken or crispy duck with wilted spinach and fried sage leaves.

note

Feta cheese is, of course, Greek or Cypriot, not Italian, but goes very well in this salad.

seafood

swedish crayfish party

August is crayfish season in Sweden, when the stores are full of special crayfish party paraphernalia—paper hats, paper lanterns with sunny faces, and candles for the table, even though the summer evenings are long and light. These crayfish are sometimes called crawdads, but if unavailable the dish is equally good made with large shrimp. Serve with toast or crusty bread—plus good butter, glasses of icy aquavit (or vodka if you can't find it), and cold beer. Such a party is always for a big group, 6–8 people at least: serve 10–20 crayfish each, depending on size.

To cook the crayfish, start the day before. Put the salt, dill seed, and bundle of dill in a large saucepan, add 2½ quarts water and bring to a rolling boil. Add the crayfish 5–6 at a time to the boiling water. Cover with a lid and simmer for 5 minutes, or just until they turn red. Like all seafood, they shouldn't be cooked too long or they will be tough.

Remove the crayfish with a slotted spoon and transfer to a large bowl. Tuck more fresh dill between them. Put the saucepan in a bowl of cold water to bring down the temperature quickly. When a little cooler, strain the liquid over the crayfish and let cool completely. Keep in the refrigerator overnight or up to 24 hours.

If using ready-cooked crayfish or shrimp, put them in the bowl with fresh dill. Boil the water with salt, dill seeds, and bunch of dill, let cool, then strain over the crayfish and chill as before.

When ready to serve, drain the crayfish and pile generously onto a large serving platter. Top with the bunch of dill and serve with toast or bread, lots of good butter for spreading, aquavit or vodka, and beer. Provide lobster crackers and picks, big table napkins (I use white dish towels), and finger bowls.

To eat the crayfish, remove its claws and crack them. Eat the meat with your fingers. Pull off the tail and cut it down the side. Pull out the tail meat and remove and discard the dark thread. Eat on buttered toast or bread—or all alone. I like to serve them with a bowl of mayonnaise for dipping, but it's not traditional.

note

To serve iced aquavit, most Scandinavian households have a special decanter with dimpled sides. The liquor is decanted into the bottle and put in the freezer. Aquavit glasses are very elegant, like mini martini glasses.

10–20 uncooked crayfish or shrimp per person
1 recipe Classic Mayonnaise (page 22), (optional)

dill marinade

2 tablespoons sea salt
3 tablespoons dill seed
a large bunch of fresh dill, tied up with kitchen twine

to serve

a small bunch of fresh dill, preferably with flower heads
toast or crusty bread
unsalted butter
iced aquavit or vodka
beer

serves 4–6

greek octopus salad

This was one of my favorite summer salads when I lived in Sydney. The Sydney Fish Market, now a huge tourist attraction, used to be run by Greek fishermen, and Greeks are in love with octopus and squid. Octopus in Greece is banged against the ancient stone quay by handsome fellows straight out of *Shirley Valentine*. In Sydney, the octopus are put in a concrete mixer with a few shovels of ice and churned until tender. If you have a Greek fishmonger, he will remove the beak, eyes, and insides. Otherwise—it's very easy.

1–2 octopus, cleaned (2–4 lb. total)

1 large potato, peeled but left whole

3 garlic cloves, crushed

a sprig of fresh oregano

2–3 sprigs of dill

green herb dressing (quantities depend on size of octopus!)

5–6 tablespoons extra virgin olive oil

freshly squeezed juice of 1/2–1 lemon

sea salt and freshly ground black pepper

a handful of basil, sliced

leaves from a sprig of oregano, chopped

1 tablespoon chopped fresh dill

to serve

sprigs of basil

sprigs of dill

2 tablespoons chopped fresh parsley

serves 8–10

Put the octopus in a large saucepan, bring to a boil, add the potato, garlic, oregano, and dill, and return to a boil. Reduce the heat and simmer until the potato is cooked. When it is cooked, so is the octopus: it will take about 30 minutes.

Remove the octopus from the pot (you can use the juice for a soup, but discard if making a salad). Rub off the skin (if preferred) and remove the suckers. Cut the octopus into bite-size pieces.

Put the dressing ingredients in a large bowl and beat with a fork. Add the octopus and toss to coat. Chill until ready to serve, topped with basil, dill and parsley.

notes

• To clean a large octopus, turn it upside down so the tentacles form a star. In the middle of the star is the hard beak. Cut it out and discard. Make a slit down the body of the beast and rinse out the guts. There is a quill inside (like a piece of transparent plastic)—remove it and give it to your budgie.

• If you don't want to cook the octopus whole, prepare it like a squid. Pull off the tentacles—the insides should come out too. Cut the tentacles off just above their join, so they make a star. Cut out the beak as before. Rinse out the body. Keep the tentacles and body and discard the rest.

mussels in ice wine

This way of cooking mussels is one of my favorite summer salads. It is based on the traditional recipe of mussels in white wine and garlic and I discovered it more or less by mistake. I was cooking a large quantity of mussels for a lunch party, opening them in batches, then stopping them cooking by putting them on a bed of ice. Originally, I used a fruity, oaky Australian wine—but I have also tried this with mirin and sake (which is fabulous) and with grated ginger added and without the thyme or bay leaf. Note—don't add salt until you've tasted the dressing at the end. Mussel juice is very sea-salty and will probably have all the salt you need.

Put a layer of ice cubes in a small roasting dish and put a rack on top.

Put the wine, garlic, onion, thyme, bay leaf, and parsley in a large saucepan and bring to a boil. Working in batches, add the prepared mussels, put on the lid, and let steam until they open—just a minute or two each. Remove as they do so, take the empty shell off the top and put the mussel in its bottom shell on the rack over ice. Repeat until all have opened. When the mussels are cool, cover with plastic wrap and keep in the refrigerator until ready to serve. Check from time to time that the melted ice isn't flooding them—pour it off if it does, so the water doesn't dilute the mussel flavor.

Strain the cooking liquid, let cool, then chill. It may be gritty, so strain through cheesecloth if necessary. Put a serving platter in the freezer.

When ready to serve, spread a layer of ice cubes on the platter and arrange the mussels on top. Strew snipped chives over the mussels, then spoon the cooking liquid over the top. I think a sauce squeeze bottle would be useful for this—you need a little dressing in each shell.

note

To prepare mussels, rinse them under cold running water. Scrub off any mud with a small brush and discard any that seem heavy (they will be full of mud). If you like, you can scrape off any large barnacles, but they don't matter—they simply indicate that your mussels are free range. Pull off and discard any wiry beards. Tap each mussel against the work surface and discard any that don't close (that means it's dead). After cooking, discard any that haven't opened.

4 lb. large mussels (see note)

1 cup fruity white wine, such as chardonnay

3 garlic cloves, crushed

1 small onion, chopped

a sprig of thyme

1 bay leaf

2 sprigs of parsley

a handful of chives, snipped

serves 4–6

spicy thai shrimp salad

This salad is very simple—you can also make it with precooked shrimp. I cut them in half lengthwise, so they're easier to eat, but also, when stir-frying they curl into pretty corkscrews. When preparing the lemongrass and kaffir lime leaves, make sure to slice them very thinly indeed. If you can't find them, use a squeeze of lemon juice and some grated regular lime zest instead. The grated zest of kaffir limes is much more scented and delicious than that of regular limes, which can be used if you can't find the real thing. *Kaffir* is a Hindi word meaning "foreign," so throughout history people have thought these limes looked a little unusual.

1 tablespoon peanut oil

1 tablespoon red Thai curry paste

12 uncooked shrimp, shelled, deveined, and halved lengthwise

12 cherry tomatoes, halved

a handful of mint sprigs, to serve

spicy thai dressing

1 stalk of lemongrass, outer leaves discarded, remainder very finely chopped

2 red bird chiles, thinly sliced and seeded if preferred

2 pink Thai shallots or 1 small regular shallot, thinly sliced lengthwise

1 tablespoon brown sugar or palm sugar

freshly squeezed juice of 2 unwaxed limes

grated zest of 2 kaffir limes

a handful of fresh cilantro, finely chopped

3 scallions, finely chopped

2 kaffir lime leaves, mid-rib removed, the leaves very thinly sliced crosswise, then finely chopped

serves 4

Heat the oil and curry paste in a wok, add the shrimp, and stir-fry for about 1 minute until opaque. Let cool.

To make the dressing, rush the lemongrass, 1 chile, and half the shallots with a mortar and pestle. Add the sugar, lime juice, and zest and mix well until the sugar dissolves. Stir in the remaining chile and shallots, and the cilantro, scallions, and lime leaves.

Put the shrimp into a serving bowl, add the cherry tomatoes, pour the dressing over the top, and toss well. Serve, topped with mint.

variations

• This dressing is also good with crab claws—stir-fried or boiled.

• Use scallops instead of shrimp.

• Try other Thai curry pastes, or a mixture of peanut oil and toasted sesame oil.

salade niçoise

Salade Niçoise is one of the classic composed salads. There has been much pontificating about the most authentic ingredients, but I think you can really use whatever you like from the basic list. Niçoise always seems to include tuna or anchovies or both; lettuce or tomatoes or both; eggs or potatoes or both; green beans or olives or both. They used to be arranged artistically in concentric circles on a large platter, but these days, more modern abstract forms in single servings seem to be in fashion. A wonderful lunch for four or an appetizer for eight.

Cook the baby potatoes in boiling salted water until tender, about 10 minutes. Drain and plunge them in a bowl of ice water with ice cubes. Let cool. Drain, then toss in a little olive oil and cut in half.

Put the eggs in a saucepan of cold water, bring to a boil, reduce the heat, and simmer for 5 minutes. Drain, then cover with cold water. When cool, peel, then cut in half just before serving.

Steam the fava beans and green beans separately until tender. Plunge into ice water, then pop each fava bean out of its gray skin. Alternatively, microwave the fava beans on HIGH for 3 minutes if fresh or 2 minutes if frozen, then refresh in ice water and peel as before. Microwave the green beans for 2 minutes, then plunge into the ice water as before.

Blanch the scallions for 30 seconds in boiling water. Drain and plunge into the ice water. Alternatively, leave uncooked, but trim and halve lengthwise.

Finely slice the red onions and cucumbers, preferably on a mandoline—slice the cucumbers diagonally. If peeling the bell peppers, do so using a vegetable peeler, then cut off the top and bottom, open out, seed, and cut the flesh into thick strips.

Put the lettuce leaves on a platter. Add bundles of green beans and scallions, then the potatoes, halved eggs, tomatoes, cucumber, onions, and peppers. Top with anchovies or tuna, black olives, caperberries or capers, and basil leaves. Mix the vinaigrette ingredients in a small pitcher and serve separately.

note

You can tie up the bundles of green beans with blanched scallion leaves.

10–12 small salad potatoes, such as fingerlings

4 small eggs

1 cup shelled fava beans or baby lima beans, fresh or frozen, or 6 cooked baby artichokes, halved

4 oz. green beans, trimmed

3 scallions, halved lengthwise

2 small red onions, halved lengthwise

2 Kirby cucumbers or 8 inches regular cucumber, unwaxed

2 red or yellow bell peppers, peeled (see method)

4 romaine heart leaves or other crisp lettuce leaves

1 basket cherry tomatoes, about 20, halved

1 small can anchovies, drained

1 large can or jar of good-quality tuna packed in olive oil, drained

about 20 Niçoise black olives

about 20 caperberries or 3 tablespoons salt-packed capers, rinsed and drained

a large handful of fresh basil leaves

olive oil, for tossing the potatoes

vinaigrette

1/3 cup extra virgin olive oil

1 tablespoon white wine vinegar, cider vinegar, or sherry vinegar

1 teaspoon Dijon mustard (optional)

1 garlic clove, crushed

sea salt and freshly ground black pepper

serves 8 as an appetizer, 4 as an entrée

tonno e fagioli

Tonno e fagioli—tuna and beans. I love this simple, delicious antipasti, discovered on my first trip to Italy, when every single thing I saw, heard, and ate etched itself into my brain as the epitome of pleasure. Now I make it when I come home from work, all the stores have shut, and I've run out of almost everything. Though any dolphin-friendly canned tuna is fine, it will be fabulously good if you use top-quality French or Italian tuna—it will blow the budget of course, but why not! Cannellini beans can be delicate, so toss them gently. Though not traditional, I've also made this with chickpeas, lentils, pinto beans, and green flageolets, and use canned salmon instead of tuna sometimes. Easy, adaptable, and good.

Put the garlic on a chopping board, crush with the flat of a knife, add a large pinch of salt, then mash to a paste with the tip of the knife. Transfer to a bowl, add the vinegar and 2 tablespoons of the oil, and beat with a fork.

Add the beans and onions and toss gently. Taste, then add extra olive oil and vinegar to taste.

Drain the tuna and separate into large chunks. Add to the bowl and turn gently to coat with the dressing. Top with the basil and cracked black pepper.

note

For salads and dressings, I prefer young garlic. The older and drier it is, the more peppery it will become, so you will need less.

1–2 large garlic cloves, crushed

1 tablespoon sherry vinegar or white wine vinegar

1/3 cup extra virgin olive oil

4 cups cooked or canned cannellini or other white beans (2 cans, 15 oz. each) rinsed and drained

2 red onions, finely sliced into petals, then blanched,* or 6 small scallions, sliced

14 oz. can or jar of best-quality tuna

a few handfuls of basil

sea salt and freshly ground black pepper

serves 6

Blanching is optional, but I think it takes the edge off the sharpness of the onions.

meat and poultry

french duck salade tiède

This is one of the classics of French cooking and a perfect example of what they call *salade tiède* or warm salad. It includes bitter leaves such as spinach, frisée, and escarole, and the salad is topped with crisp bacon, in this case the French *lardons*, or thick bacon bits. The cooking juices from the pine nuts, garlic, and bacon are used to dress the salad. Without the duck, it can be served as an appetizer, or as an accompaniment to an entrée. Many thanks to my friend, author, and Michelin-starred chef Sonia Stevenson for teaching me this foolproof way of cooking duck breasts, which produces lots of wonderful duck fat for sautéing potatoes later.

Put the duck breasts skin-side down in a skillet lightly brushed with olive oil. Sprinkle the flesh side with a little sea salt. Cook gently over low heat for 20–30 minutes to render out the fat—you will have to pour it off from time to time into a heatproof bowl. Take it slowly—the skin will gradually become crisp and golden and the fat line will almost disappear.

Turn the duck over and cook at a high heat just to brown the flesh side—the interior should remain rare. Remove from the pan and let rest for about 5 minutes if serving hot, or 20 minutes if serving cool. Carve crosswise on a wooden board, making sure each slice has its share of crackling.

Put the spinach in a bowl, add the vinaigrette, and toss lightly. Divide the leaves between 4 dinner plates or 8 appetizer plates.

Meanwhile, rinse and dry the skillet. Reheat, add about 2 tablespoons olive oil, then the pine nuts. Toast over low heat, tossing gently, until golden on all sides, about 1 minute. Take care—they burn easily. Remove from the pan and let cool on a plate. Add the garlic to the pan and sauté gently until crisp and golden brown. Remove to the same plate.

Add the bacon lardons and sauté gently until crispy. Add the lardons to the salads, top with the pine nuts and garlic, then spoon the hot scented oil from the pan over the salads. Add freshly ground black pepper and serve.

variation

This is also good with pan-fried chicken livers.

4 duck breasts

1 lb. baby spinach leaves

¼ cup Vinaigrette (page 21), traditionally made with red wine vinegar

about 3 oz. pine nuts, 1 cup

3 garlic cloves, finely sliced

8 oz. bacon lardons, pancetta cubes, or finely sliced smoked prosciutto, as fatty as possible

sea salt and freshly ground black pepper

olive oil, for sautéing

serves 4 as an entrée, 8 as an appetizer

vietnamese duck salad
with table salad herbs

You can use any cooked meat for this salad. In Chinatown, you can buy marvelous barbecued duck (and pork). The ducks are sold whole, halved, or quartered. Just don't let the cook chop it up into chunks—it's better if you pull the duck off the bones in long shreds. Alternatively, butchers sell pairs of duck legs quite cheaply—everyone wants the breasts. So—if you rub them with a little salt and pepper, then roast them until the skin is crispy, they make a great salad. You can use them to make a French or American-style salad, but I like this one, based on the traditional Vietnamese chicken and peanut salad, made of stir-fried ground chicken.

2 duck legs

4 handfuls of bean sprouts, rinsed and drained

1 young carrot

6 scallions, halved, then thinly sliced lengthwise

a handful of fresh mint leaves, preferably Vietnamese mint

a handful of Asian basil leaves (optional)

1 recipe Vietnamese Chile-Lime Dressing (page 25)

2 tablespoons pan-toasted peanuts, finely chopped

sea salt and freshly ground black pepper

serves 4

Rub the duck with salt and pepper and put in a preheated oven at 400°F or higher. Roast until the skin is crisp and the meat tender, about 45 minutes–1 hour.

When cooked, remove and set aside until cool enough to handle. Pull the meat and crispy skin off the bones and discard the bones or keep them for stock. Try to use freshly cooked duck for salads, but if you must refrigerate it, reheat it before using. (Most meats, but especially fatty ones, are nicer if warm or cool, not cold.)

To trim the bean sprouts, pinch off the tails and remove the bean from between the two leaves (optional).

To prepare the carrot, peel and shred into long matchsticks on a mandoline or the large blade of a box grater.

Pile the bean sprouts onto 4 plates. Add the carrot and duck and top with the scallions, mint, and basil leaves, if using. Sprinkle with the Chile-Lime Dressing, toss to coat, top with the toasted peanuts, then serve.

variation

You may also add bean thread noodles to this salad. Soak about 1 oz. noodles in a bowl of hot water for 15 minutes, then drain and chop into short lengths with kitchen shears. Keep in cold water until ready to serve, then drain before adding to the salad.

insalata gonzaga

A lovely, simple chicken salad named after the Gonzaga Dukes of Mantua, near Modena, the home of balsamic vinegar. True balsamic vinegar is rare and expensive, but use the best you can afford. This recipe comes from my Italian cousin, Tina Valentino-Capezza, who found this recipe in Milan.

Put the pine nuts in a dry skillet and heat gently until lightly golden. Take care—they burn easily. Remove to a plate and let cool.

Put the chicken and radicchio in a bowl and toss gently. Sprinkle with sea salt, then with the vinegar. Toss gently with your hands. Sprinkle with olive oil and toss again. Taste, then add extra salt, vinegar, or oil, as you wish.

Transfer to salad plates, sprinkle with the raisins, pine nuts, pepper, and a few drops of balsamic vinegar and top with shards of Parmesan.

note

• For this salad, I soaked the raisins in verjuice for 10 minutes before adding to the salad. Verjuice is halfway between vinegar and wine, and can be found in gourmet stores. Omit if unavailable.

• Note this Italian method of dressing salads—sprinkle first with salt, then with vinegar, toss, then sprinkle with oil. Taste, then, if necessary, add extra of any ingredient to balance the flavors.

• If you prefer peppery leaves rather than bitter ones, this salad is also good with watercress instead of radicchio.

about 3 oz. pine nuts, 1 cup

8 oz. cooked boneless chicken, preferably breast, pulled into long shreds

1–2 heads of radicchio, leaves separated

1 tablespoon red wine vinegar, or to taste

1/3 cup cold-pressed extra virgin olive oil, or to taste

1/4 cup raisins, soaked in hot water for 10 minutes

1–2 tablespoons balsamic vinegar

sea salt and freshly cracked black pepper

4 oz. fresh Parmesan cheese at room temperature, cut into shards with a vegetable peeler

serves 4

warm chicken salad
with harissa dressing

Everyone loves a chicken salad—but it depends on the chicken. Roasted is gorgeous, poached is very good, and grilled is best of all. The main thing, I think, is that the salad should be prepared while the chicken is still warm. Don't take a chilled, cooked chicken breast and chop it into bits. Not nice. Take the same breast, just after it's been cooked, and pull it into large pieces. It separates along the grain and tastes better and is more tender.

2 baskets ripe cherry tomatoes, or 4 vine-ripened clusters of cherry tomatoes, such as Juliette or Elfin

½ garlic clove, crushed

4 freshly cooked chicken breasts

salad greens

20 large green or black olives, pitted and halved

2 red onions, halved, then cut into thin wedges lengthwise

sea salt and freshly ground black pepper

harissa dressing

⅓ cup extra virgin olive oil

1 tablespoon harissa paste

1 tablespoon cider or sherry vinegar

a baking sheet

serves 4

Put the tomatoes on a baking sheet—if using vine tomatoes, put the whole vine on the sheet. Sprinkle with salt and olive oil, plus crushed garlic, and roast in a preheated oven at 400°F or higher, until slightly charred and starting to collapse. Let cool, but do not chill.

Mix the dressing ingredients in a salad bowl and beat with a fork.

While still warm, pull the chicken into long chunks. Add to the bowl, then add the greens, olives, and onions and toss gently in the dressing.

Pile onto salad plates, add the tomatoes, and serve.

notes

• Pit and halve the olives yourself. Somehow, olives just taste better when you buy them with their pits in. Choose any kind—with garlic, chile, lemon, and herbs—whatever looks good on the day.

• I love dressings made with smoky, spicy harissa paste. Brands vary in heat, so add a little, taste, then add more if you prefer. Alternatively, you might like regular mustard instead.

turkey cobb salad

This American classic was invented in the Roaring Twenties by a California restaurateur of the same name. It's essentially a "bitser" salad—bitser this and bitser that—just like Niçoise or Gado Gado, two other legendary mixed salads. It's also a good post-turkey dish, when you have lots of turkey left over and you're looking for an effortless way to serve it. I always use the fattiest bacon or prosciutto—I can't see the point of bacon with no fat. Traditionally, the ingredients were arranged in lines. I've never liked that. Tumble it together. The dressing is not traditional, but I use it instead of mayonnaise—it is light and marvelous.

4 slices fatty bacon

2 Hass avocados

1 large head Bibb or Boston lettuce

6 ripe plum tomatoes, cut into wedges

1 lb. cooked turkey, pulled into large shreds (page 17), at room temperature

2 hard-cooked eggs, quartered

4 oz. Roquefort cheese, cut into thin slices, or crumbled

olive oil, for cooking

lemon cream dressing

1 cup heavy cream

freshly squeezed juice of 1 lemon

a handful of chives, chopped

to serve

crusty rolls

small cornichons, halved lengthwise, or sliced pickles

serves 4

Brush a skillet with olive oil, add the bacon, and cook until crispy but not crumbly. Remove and drain on crumpled paper towels.

Cut the avocados in half, remove the seeds, then scoop out the flesh with a teaspoon.

Share the bacon, lettuce, tomatoes, turkey, eggs, cheese, and avocado between 4 plates or bowls.

To make the dressing, put the cream in a bowl, add the lemon juice, and beat well. Stir in the chives, then spoon over the salad and serve with crusty rolls and cornichons.

note

Of course you can use the traditional regular vinaigrette with this recipe (page 21).

rare beef salad
with wasabi and watercress

A splendid special-occasion salad for a summer lunch party. When you serve it, cut the beef into thick slices, like steak. For the best flavor, let the meat return to room temperature first (it only takes a few minutes). Increase the amount of fillet to cater for the number of guests—since it's the same thickness, it will take the same time in the oven, no matter how big it is. Don't salt it first, or you'll draw out the juices. I like top-quality beef like this to be cooked absolutely plain, with any flavorings coming from the accompaniments. Wasabi is one of my favorite fiery condiments (I like it better than horseradish), because its spice is short, sharp, and very strong.

Brush a heavy roasting pan with olive oil and heat on top of the stove until very hot. Add the beef and seal on all sides until nicely browned. Transfer to a preheated oven and roast at 400°F for 20 minutes. Remove from the oven and set aside to set the juices. Sprinkle with salt and pepper.

Let the meat cool to room temperature and reserve any cooking juices. If preparing in advance, wrap closely in foil and chill, but return it to room temperature before serving.

Arrange the leaves down the middle of a rectangular or oval serving dish. Slice the beef into ½-inch-thick slices with a very sharp carving knife (or an electric knife). Arrange in overlapping slices on top of the leaves and pour any cooking juices from the roasting pan or carving board over the top.

Mix the mayonnaise with the wasabi paste and serve separately.

note

For a special-occasion dish like this, you simply must make the mayonnaise yourself. It's not difficult, especially if you have a food processor (page 22).

1 beef tenderloin, about 20 inches long, well trimmed

1 lb. watercress or other peppery leaves, such as arugula or, when in season, wild garlic (ramps)

sea salt and freshly ground black pepper

olive oil, for cooking

wasabi mayonnaise

1 recipe Classic Mayonnaise (page 22)

1 tube wasabi paste

serves 8

thai mango beef salad

The beef in this recipe is grilled but very rare. If you don't like rare meat, substitute something else, don't cook the meat until it's well done or even medium. I also like crispy roasted duck legs, poached chicken, or shrimp. The mango isn't traditional, but I like its juicy sweetness compared with the fiery chiles. Papaya is also good.

4 bundles of bean thread vermicelli noodles, about 1 oz. each (optional)

2 tablespoons dark soy sauce

1 tablespoon fish sauce

1 tablespoon brown sugar

1 lb. beef tenderloin

4 small pink Thai shallots, or 2 regular, thinly sliced

1 Kirby cucumber or 4 inches regular cucumber, thinly sliced

1 stalk of lemongrass, outer leaves removed and discarded, remainder very thinly sliced

lime dressing

¼ cup lime juice

¼ cup fish sauce

1 teaspoon brown sugar or palm sugar

to serve

1 ripe mango, peeled and cut into ½-inch cubes

2 red bird chiles, thinly sliced diagonally

2 scallions, thinly sliced

a large handful of mint leaves

serves 4

If serving with noodles, put them in a bowl and cover with hot water. Let soak for about 15 minutes, then drain. Keep in a bowl of cold water until ready to serve, then drain and cut into short lengths, about 2–4 inches, with kitchen shears.

Put the soy, fish sauce, and sugar in a bowl and beat with a fork to dissolve the sugar. Add the beef and turn to coat. Set aside for 1–2 hours to develop the flavors. When ready to cook, preheat an outdoor grill or stove-top grill pan until very hot. Put the meat on the grill or pan and cook, turning from time to time, until the surface is well browned and the middle still pink, about 5 minutes in total, depending on the thickness of the meat. Remove from the heat and set aside in a warm place for about 5 minutes to set the juices.

Put the meat on a board and slice thinly crosswise. Cut the slices into bite-size strips about 2 inches long.

To make the dressing, put the lime juice, fish sauce, and sugar in a bowl and beat with a fork to dissolve the sugar. Taste, then if you prefer add 1 tablespoon water at a time until you like the taste. Add the beef slices and any meat juices, the shallots, cucumber and lemongrass. Toss well.

Put a pile of noodles, if using, onto each plate, then add the dressed salad. Add the mango, chiles and scallions, then spoon any remaining dressing from the bowl over each serving. Top with mint leaves and serve.

note

I prefer small Kirby cucumbers, which aren't as watery as the regular kind. If you can't get them, use part of an ordinary one, but cut it in half lengthwise and scrape out the seed section before slicing. I always look for unwaxed cucumbers—if they're waxed, you'll have to peel them, which rather defeats the purpose. You can also cut 4 lengthwise strips out of the skin with a canelle knife if you yearn for more decoration.

pasta, rice, and
noodles

couscous salad
with mint and cilantro

I have yet to meet a pasta salad I could love—other than couscous. This very quick and easy salad is endlessly adaptable. Omit the chicken and add other uncooked or lightly blanched vegetables, such as cucumber, baby carrots, cherry tomatoes, sugar snap peas, asparagus tips, or herbs. Easy-cook couscous is supposed to be just soaked then drained, but I find it's better for a little more microwaving or steaming after soaking. It should be dry and fluffy.

¼ cup couscous

½ cup boiling chicken stock or water

6 semi-dried tomatoes or 6 fresh cherry tomatoes, halved

2 marinated artichoke hearts, sliced

3–4 scallions, sliced

15 oz. canned chickpeas, rinsed and drained, about 2 cups

harissa dressing

⅓ cup extra virgin olive oil

1 tablespoon sherry vinegar or cider vinegar

1 tablespoon harissa paste

sea salt and freshly ground black pepper

to serve

a handful of flat-leaf parsley, coarsely chopped

sprigs of watercress

springs of mint

sprigs of cilantro

snipped chives

serves 2

Put the couscous in a heatproof bowl and cover with the stock or water. Leave for about 15 minutes until the water has been absorbed. For a fluffier texture, put the soaked couscous in a strainer and steam over simmering water for another 10 minutes, or microwave in a jug or bowl on 50 percent for about 5 minutes. Drain if necessary, pressing the liquid through the strainer with a spoon, then fluff up with a fork. Let cool.

When ready to make up the salad, put the couscous in a bowl, add the tomatoes, artichoke hearts, scallions, and chickpeas. Keep the watercress and herbs in a separate container until just before serving.

To make the dressing, put the olive oil, vinegar, and harissa paste in a bowl and beat with a fork. Add salt and pepper to taste. Sprinkle half the dressing over the couscous mixture and toss with a fork. Add the watercress and herbs and serve. Serve the extra dressing separately for people to help themselves.

variation

This is a perfect picnic, lunchbox, or make-ahead salad. Put the watercress and herbs into a small container and seal. Put the dressing ingredients in a screw-top jar and shake to mix. Shake again just before serving. Put the couscous and remaining ingredients in a lidded plastic bowl, and seal until ready to use. To serve, add the dressing, parsley, and watercress and toss well.

chilled japanese salad
with shrimp and soba noodles

One of the great Japanese cold dishes, in which the quality and flavor of the buckwheat can be especially savored. Soba noodles are an elegant fawn color, and there is a beautiful green-tea-flavored, pale green version known as cha-soba (*cha* means "tea" in many languages). Other noodles, such as somen or thick udon noodles, are also good this way.

14 oz. dried soba noodles, brown or green

12 dried shiitake mushrooms

2 tablespoons Japanese soy sauce (tamari)

2 tablespoons mirin (Japanese sweetened rice wine) or dry sherry

12 uncooked shrimp

12 scallions, finely sliced

4 teaspoons furokaki pepper (optional)

4 teaspoons wasabi paste

ice cubes

dipping sauce

1 cup dashi stock*

2 tablespoons mirin (Japanese sweetened rice wine) or dry sherry

a pinch of sugar

3 tablespoons Japanese soy sauce (tamari)

serves 4

Dashi and other Japanese ingredients in this book are available in Japanese stores and some supermarkets. Dissolve 1 teaspoon in 1 cup hot (not boiling) water, or to taste.

Put the dipping sauce ingredients in a saucepan, bring to the boil, reduce the heat, and simmer for about 5 minutes, then chill.

Cook the noodles for 5–6 minutes or according to the package instructions. Drain, rinse in cold water, and cool over ice. Chill.

Put the shiitakes in a saucepan, cover with 1 cup boiling water, and soak until soft. Remove and discard the mushroom stems. Add the mushrooms to the pan.

Add the soy sauce and mirin to the pan, bring to a boil, and simmer for a few minutes to meld the flavors. Add the shrimp and simmer for about 1 minute until firm. Drain, reserving the cooking liquid. Shell the shrimp, but leave the tail fins intact. Devein and split each shrimp down the back to the fin, giving a butterfly shape. Chill the shrimp and poaching liquid. Just before serving, plunge the chilled noodles into the liquid, then drain.

To serve, half-fill a lacquer bowl with ice and water, then add the noodles. Serve the shrimp, scallions, and mushrooms separately. Let your guests assemble their salads themselves. Serve with separate dishes of furokaki pepper, if using, wasabi paste, and dipping sauce.

japanese tofu salad
with sesame seeds

If you're not a tofu fan, this elegant, simple recipe is where to start your love affair. It is made with silken tofu, a name that describes its texture. It should be eaten very fresh, and if you bring it home in a container with water, drain off the water and cover with fresh cold water. It will keep for several days if you change the water daily. The tofu won't fall apart so easily if you firm it up by pressing between two plates—a method I saw demonstrated by Japanese food writer Kimiko Barber at Books for Cooks in London's Notting Hill.

2 blocks silken tofu, well chilled

dipping sauce

¼ cup Japanese soy sauce (I prefer to use wheat-free tamari)

1 tablespoon sugar

¼ cup sake

1 cup dashi*

to serve

2 tablespoons white sesame seeds

2 scallions, finely sliced

2 inches fresh ginger, peeled and finely grated

serves 6

*Dashi is available in powder or concentrate form in Japanese stores and some supermarkets. Dissolve 1 teaspoon in 1 cup hot (not boiling) water, or to taste.

Put the dipping sauce ingredients in a small saucepan and heat slowly until the sugar has dissolved. Cool and chill.

Put the tofu blocks carefully on a flat plate and invert another plate over them. Put a weight, like a can of beans, on top and set aside for at least 30 minutes. Set it on a tilt on the draining board (put a chopstick under the plate) to drain out some of the moisture. Keep them cold.

Put the sesame seeds in a dry skillet and toast gently until aromatic. Do not let burn.

To serve, take a block of tofu in one hand and carefully cut in 3 both ways—you will end up with 9 cubes. Repeat with the second block of tofu. Either put all the tofu in a glass serving dish, or put 3 in each guest's bowl. Serve a small plate of sesame seeds, scallion, and grated ginger, and another bowl with the dipping sauce to each person.

black rice salad
with chile greens

I have a passion for Asian rice, with its subtle flavors and special uses. I've tried various kinds in salads and, apart from very sticky rice, most are great. My favorite is Asian black rice—if you can't find it, use wild rice. The main thing is that you should never put rice in the refrigerator. Boil it, cool it, make the salad, and serve it as fast as possible. And if you're not going to serve it straight away, put sushi vinegar through it as it's cooling, in order to flavor and preserve it. The result is utterly wonderful.

Put the dressing ingredients in a saucepan, bring to a boil, and simmer until the sugar has dissolved. Taste and add water if necessary. Cool.

To make the sushi vinegar, put the vinegar, sugar, salt, ginger, and garlic in a saucepan and simmer over low heat.

Put the rice in a saucepan, cover with water to 1 finger's joint above the top of the rice, and bring to a boil. Cover tightly with a lid, reduce the heat and simmer for 14 minutes (12 for white rice). Turn off the heat, do NOT remove the lid, and set aside for 12 minutes. Remove the lid. The rice should be perfectly fluffy. If not (and this sometimes happens with black rice), put the lid back on and boil hard for about 1 minute. Remove from the heat, drain, then run it under cold water. Drain again.

Transfer to a bowl, sprinkle with the sushi vinegar, and stir it through gently with a spoon.

Put the asparagus stalk ends in a saucepan of boiling salted water for 1½ minutes or until you can just pierce them with a fork. Scoop out and drain in a colander under cold running water. Add the tips and sugar snaps and cook as before for about 30 seconds, until just tender. Drain under cold running water. Cook the green beans and fava beans, if using, in the same way.

Put all the greens in a bowl, add the chile and scallions, and mix well.

Add the chile greens to the rice and sprinkle with the dressing. Stir gently, then serve.

note

This recipe is Asian. However, you can alter its emphasis by changing the dressing to a regular Vinaigrette (page 21) and, for instance, using red onion instead of scallion, and omitting the chile.

1¼ cups Asian black rice or your choice of other rice

asian dressing

2 stalks of lemongrass, outer leaves discarded, remainder very finely chopped

1 inch fresh ginger, peeled, grated, and juice squeezed

1 green chile, halved, seeded, and finely chopped

freshly squeezed juice of 1 lime

½ cup fish sauce

2 tablespoons brown sugar

sushi vinegar

⅔ cup Japanese rice vinegar

⅓ cup sugar

4 teaspoons salt

2 inches fresh ginger, peeled, grated, and squeezed

3 garlic cloves, crushed

chile greens

a handful of asparagus tips, halved

a handful of sugar snap peas, sliced

a handful of green beans, cut into ½-inch pieces

1 cup cooked fava beans or baby lima beans, boiled and peeled (optional)

1 jalapeño or serrano chile, seeded and chopped

4 scallions, sliced diagonally

serves 4

websites and mail order

salad plants and seeds

The Cook's Garden
Tel: 800-457-9703
www.cooksgarden.com
Organic seeds, plants, and supplies for
culinary herbs and vegetables.

Sheperd's Garden Seeds
Tel: 800-503-9626
www.whiteflowerfarm.com
A division of Litchfield, Connecticut
perennial nursery has an excellent
selection of heirloom tomato seeds.

The Natural Gardening Company
P.O. Box 750776
Petaluma, CA 94975-0776
Tel: 707-766-9303
Fax: 707-766-9747
www.naturalgardening.com
The oldest certified organic nursery in the
US. A complete organic gardening
source for plants and seeds.

Seeds of Changes
Tel: 888-762-7333
www.seedsofchange.com
Organic garden seeds and plants.

Richters
357 Highway 47
Goodwood, Ontario, Canada L0C 1A0
Tel: 905-640-6677
Fax: 905-640-6641
www.richters.com
Herb specialists.

Penn Herb Co., Ltd.
603 North 2nd Street
Philadelphia, PA 19123
Tel: 800-523-9971
Fax: 215-632-7945
www.pennherb.com

organic meats, poultry, fish, and vegetables

Urban Organic
Tel: 888-428-8680
www.urbanorganic.net
The largest organic produce home delivery
service in America.

Pipestone Family Farms
Pipestone, Minnesota
Tel: 866-767-8875
www.pipestonefamilyfarms.com
Quality pork products from cooperative
venture of over 250 hog farmers.

Prather Ranch
Macdoel, California
Tel: 877-570-2333
www.pratherranch.com
Certified organic beef available online and
at farmers' markets in the Northern
California and Southern Oregon areas.
Call for a schedule.

Niman Ranch
Marin County, California
Tel: 510-808-0340
www.nimanranch.com
Top-quality beef, pork, and lamb. Shipped
fresh, never frozen. Available online and at
gourmet food stores all over the country.
Check website for distributors.

Eberly Poultry
1095 Mt. Airy Road
Stevens, PA 17578
Tel: 717-336-6440
Fax: 717-336-6905
www.eberlypoultry.com
Top-quality organic chicken, duck, geese,
gamebirds, and rabbits.

Wild Edibles
89 East 42nd Street
(inside Grand Central Station)
New York, NY 10017-5503
Tel: 212-687-4255
Retail store offering impeccable selection
of fresh fish and shellfish.

Browne Trading Company
Merrill's Wharf, 260 Commercial Street
Portland, Maine 04101
Tel: 207-766-2403
Fax: 207-766-2404
Mail order: 800-944-7848
www.browne-trading.com
Mail order source for superb fresh fish and
shellfish, caviar, and smoked salmon.

international ingredients

ASIAN
Pacific Rim Gourmet
11251 Coloma Road, Suite A
Gold River, CA 95670
Tel: 800-618-7575 / 916-852-7855
(outside continental U.S.)
Fax: 916-852-7911
www.pacificrim-gourmet.com
Online gourmet resource for the exotic
ingredients of the Pacific Rim, such as
bamboo steamers, rice cookers, clay pots,
hot pots, rice baskets, mortars and pestles,
cast iron woks, and sushi supplies.

Thai Grocer
2961 N. Sheridan Rd.
Chicago, IL, 60657
Tel: 773-988-8424
Fax:773-871-3969
www.thaigrocer.com

Katagiri
224 East 59th Street
New York, NY 10022
Tel: 212-755-3566
Fax: 212-752-4197
www.katagiri.com
Retail store and mail-order company
specializing in Japanese ingredients.

Kalustyan's
123 Lexington Avenue
New York, NY 10016
Tel: 212-685-3451
Fax: 212-683-8458
www.kalustyans.com
"If we don't have it, it doesn't exist."

Kam Man Food Products
200 Canal Street
New York, NY 10013
Tel: 212-571-0330
Asian foods supermarket and housewares
store in New York City's Chinatown.

Uwajimaya
Tel: 206-624-3215
www.uwajimaya.com
Large Asian grocers in Pacific Northwest—
products from China, Japan, Korea, the
Philippines, and other Asian countries. Call
for retail store locations.

www.asiafoods.com
Tel: 877-902-0841
Online source for Asian ingredients and
cooking equipment.

www.namaste.com
Tel: 866-438-4642
Online source for Indian groceries and
ingredients.

MIDDLE EASTERN
Sultan's Delight
P.O. Box 90302
Brooklyn, NY 11209
Tel: 800-852-5046
Fax: 718-745-2563
www.sultansdelight.com

www.ethnicgrocer.com
Tel: 866-438-4642
Online source for international ingredients,
recipes, and cookware.

LATIN AMERICAN
Kitchen Market
218 Eighth Avenue
New York, NY 10011
Tel: 888-468-4433
www.kitchenmarket.com
Retail store and mail order source for
chiles, spices, and other Mexican
specialties.

www.mexgrocer.com
Tel: 877-463-9476
Online grocery store for authentic
Mexican food.

index

conversion chart

Weights and measures have been rounded up
or down slightly to make measuring easier.

volume equivalents

American	Metric	Imperial
1 teaspoon	5 ml	
1 tablespoon	5 ml	
¼ cup	60 ml	2 fl. oz.
⅓ cup	75 ml	2½ fl. oz.
½ cup	125 ml	4 fl. oz.
⅔ cup	150 ml	5 fl. oz. (¼ pint)
¾ cup	175 ml	6 fl. oz.
1 cup	250 ml	8 fl. oz.

weight equivalents

Imperial	Metric		measurements	
			Inches	Cm
1 oz.	25 g		¼ inch	5 mm
2 oz.	50 g		½ inch	1 cm
3 oz.	75 g		¾ inch	1.5 cm
4 oz.	125 g		1 inch	2.5 cm
5 oz.	150 g		2 inches	5 cm
6 oz.	175 g		3 inches	7 cm
7 oz.	200 g		4 inches	10 cm
8 oz. (½ lb.)	250 g		5 inches	12 cm
9 oz.	275 g		6 inches	15 cm
10 oz.	300 g		7 inches	18 cm
11 oz.	325 g		8 inches	20 cm
12 oz.	375 g		9 inches	23 cm
13 oz.	400 g		10 inches	25 cm
14 oz.	425 g		11 inches	28 cm
15 oz.	475 g		12 inches	30 cm
16 oz. (1 lb.)	500 g			
2 1b.	1 kg			

oven temperatures

110°C	(225°F)	Gas ¼
120°C	(250°F)	Gas ½
140°C	(275°F)	Gas 1
150°C	(300°F)	Gas 2
160°C	(325°F)	Gas 3
180°C	(350°F)	Gas 4
190°C	(375°F)	Gas 5
200°C	(400°F)	Gas 6
220°C	(425°F)	Gas 7
230°C	(450°F)	Gas 8
240°C	(475°F)	Gas 9